COLLECTING THINGS

ELIZABETH GUNDREY

A Piccolo Original

PAN BOOKS LTD
LONDON AND SYDNEY

First published 1974 by Pan Books Ltd,
Cavaye Place, London SW10 9PG

ISBN 0 330 24067 6

Printed in Great Britain by
Richard Clay (The Chaucer Press), Ltd, Bungay, Suffolk

INTRODUCTION

COLLECTOMANIA is a disease that gets all of us sooner or later. This book will only make it worse, because it has lots of ideas for over a hundred things you might enjoy hunting down and then arranging.

Collecting is fun because, first of all, there's quite a bit of detective work to do before you find what you're after. It's fun because you make new friends: you come across other people with the same interest as yourself; you begin trading 'swaps'; and even non-collecting friends will get drawn in – when they know what you're after, they'll start making you presents of things for your collection. You might start a collectors' club among your friends. You'll learn an awful lot as you go along and maybe become a real expert one day.

The things in this book are not difficult or expensive to get, and they don't take up too much room at home. Some are good for wall displays (using Blu-Tack, 'magic mounts' or double-sided Sellotape to fix them without harming the walls), some go into scrapbooks, and other tiny ones could be sorted and stored in plastic egg-boxes or in miniature 'chests-of-drawers' made by gluing matchboxes together; you can make the drawer-pulls with brass paperclips (the sort with a round head and two spikes – push the spikes through the matchbox from the outside and open them flat on the inside). Page 49 tells you how to make a home museum from a collection, and there are other display ideas on page 106.

If you want to take up any of the natural history ones seriously, get *The Naturalist's Handbook* by Geoffrey Watson, also published in Piccolo. But you'll notice this book does *not* recommend collecting birds' eggs or butterflies: to collect these is to destroy life, and already too many beautiful wild creatures are becoming rare or vanishing altogether. You could join the Young Zoologists Club (London Zoo, Regent's Park, London NW1) for £1: this gives you six free tickets to London Zoo and Whipsnade Zoo (Bedfordshire), a magazine three times a year, film shows, zoo tours, competitions, a badge, etc.

There are lots of other things to collect. Even those in this book are only a fraction of what's possible. You might prefer to collect record sleeves, or concert programmes if you're musical, skulls and bones of wild animals if you live in the country – or abandoned birds' nests – conjuring tricks if you've deft fingers, flotsam and jetsam if you live near the sea and can go beachcombing, fabric scraps if you're good at sewing and would like to try appliqué or patchwork, football programmes if you're keen on the game, sweet wrappers for collages if you are artistically inclined.

Now that Britain is changing to metric, old weights and measuring things (from rulers to jugs) in inches and pints will soon become rarities worth collecting.

No matter what you decide to collect, it's pretty certain that there will be at least one book on the subject, possibly a magazine for collectors and maybe a collectors' club to join if you become really keen. How to find out? Ask in the reference or children's section of your local library. And write to Shire Publications (12B Temple Square, Aylesbury, Bucks) for their list of books: they have dozens on collecting subjects, mostly 30p each, which will give you ideas. 'Ladybird' is another series of books with lots of useful titles (their address is Wills and Hepworth, Loughborough). The 'How and Why' books on natural history, etc, come from Transworld (57 Uxbridge Road, London W5).

And if you want to find shops, or mail-order people with catalogues, specializing in your chosen items, buy a copy of *Exchange and Mart* weekly (5p) and look there. Or look in *Collectors' London*: (edited by Atterbury and Eley and published by Nicholson).

Finally, if you collect something that's not in this book, I'd love to hear from you. Do write and tell me all about it, and what you do with your collection. (But first check with the index that your idea isn't already among the 150 collectable things mentioned in this book!)

Elizabeth Gundrey,
Piccolo,
Pan Books Ltd,
Cavaye Place,
London, SW10 9PG

COLLECTING THINGS

The most obvious kind of autograph-collecting is from living celebrities. You can, as the opportunity arises, queue up at stage-doors and so forth in the hope that they may sign your book when they come out. If you have a photo of the celebrity, a book or a record of his, a theatre programme, etc, for him to sign, he is more likely to do so. If not, at least offer a clean and attractive little autograph book – and have a pen ready for him, too. If you write to a celebrity for his autograph, send him a stamped envelope addressed to yourself for his reply. If you write a really interesting letter, you may even get an interesting answer back, too. Your collection of autographs could one day be really valuable if you specialize – for instance, collecting autographs of all the famous ballet-dancers (if ballet interests you) and also of younger ones who may become stars later. If you want to write to a famous person but don't know his address, here's how to get your letter to him. Write to him at the address of his publisher (if he has written a book), record company (if he has made a record), theatre or film company (if he is an actor), sports ground (if he is a player), etc.

Another interesting kind of autograph book is the one you keep for friends, if you persuade each one to do more than sign his name. A favourite poem from one, a drawing by another, a pressed flower from someone's garden, a riddle – something different on each page.

What about a 'trades' autograph book? You could collect the signatures of your milkman, postman, teacher, coalman, grocer, parson, fishmonger, policeman, doctor, etc. Then you could do a small drawing of each one at his work on the same page. The fun would be in trying to collect as many trades and professions as possible.

If you enjoy wearing them, you might like collecting them too. Just think what a lot there are – not just the plastic badges or stick-on ones you often find given away, but more important ones of brass, bronze, white or black metal. There are cap and arm badges of the Army, Navy and Air Force; nurses' badges; car or bike badges; school badges; key-ring badges; tie-clips or cuff-links with badges on them; football badges; the cap or shoulder badges worn by bus and train workers (see page 100); even teaspoons and bracelet-charms are sometimes made with badges on. Grown-up friends may have some of these they no longer want, or you can buy them (there are a number of badge shops, many of which advertise weekly in the *Exchange and Mart*).

Uniform badges of gold or silver wire and coloured threads are very cheap to buy and would make a sumptuous collection. Or you could specialize in colourful embroidered arm badges from the various public services and armed forces, here and overseas. Or buttons with regimental crests on them.

To display your badges or buttons, you can buy from a wallpaper shop some ceiling tiles of expanded polystyrene – soft, white, plastic stuff. You will find that a gentle push is enough to lodge the badge in position.

There are plenty of books, especially about Army badges. A good one to start with is *Discovering British Military Badges and Buttons* (Wilkinson-Latham, published by Shire).

····≫══ *BOOKS* ══≪····
(*and newspapers*)

Book-collecting is something you probably do already, and will probably do all your life. For any shelf full of books is a collection of sorts. You can build up a collection of your favourite author (or illustrator), or of books on a favourite subject – horses, ballet, wild-life, whatever you happen to be keen on. How is your row of Piccolos doing? You can get a free list of all the latest titles by writing to Pan Books Ltd, Cavaye Place, London SW10 9PG and see which ones you want to get next.

Some people collect old books, not new ones – the older the better; and certain books are now so rare that they cost hundreds or even thousands of pounds. But a lot of fun can be had searching through the cheap bargain trays of secondhand book shops, on junk stalls, at jumble sales and so forth, looking for long-forgotten books which have a charm all of their own. For a few pence you can find volumes of old encyclopedias, old-fashioned children's books, or bound volumes of magazines. You could decide on a particular subject – like ships, or trains, or historical costume – and make a special collection. What about old maps and atlases? Or books containing interesting prints (see page 84).

Newspapers and magazines are often thrown away, yet you might find old ones fascinating. Can you get any for the year when you were born? What other important events occurred that year, and what were fashions like then – how did your mother dress in those days? Or go back still further in time and find magazines and papers from your grandparents' childhood; when you show your collection to them they will tell you what it was like to be growing up then.

You might like to make a collection of advertisements from old magazines. How very quaint they seem now! Some are shown opposite.

When you find a new book that you like, it may be one of a big series you could collect. Write to the publishers for a list. (Their names and addresses will be inside the book.) For example, in the introduction to this book you will find the addresses of publishers who have series of books useful to young collectors. So you could start by collecting books on collecting.

I know one antique shop that sells nothing but old bottles (in Alston, Cumberland), and there are plenty of museum displays devoted to them. So bottle-collecting is a serious business.

But anyone can make a start, looking for cast-offs in sheds, attics, at the bottom of the garden and on any piece of land where people throw rubbish. If you are by the sea, you can search for castaways on beaches after a storm has tossed them ashore. Just think of the variety there is: drinks bottles, scent bottles, fruit-preserving jars, pill and medicine bottles (be sure these are thoroughly washed out if you collect them), pickle and sauce bottles.

Amber, green, blue, red, brown – their colours look fabulous, particularly if you can get someone to put up glass shelves for your collection, either in front of a window or under a light. Plain ones could be filled with water slightly tinted with coloured inks, or with marbles, or with your shell or pebble collections (see pages 94 and 88).

Some bottles have moulded decorations, others have strange shapes, curious stoppers, or unusual necks. Many have words embossed on them. You might make a separate collection of their labels (see page 58).

Your collection could well include such things as a very old soda siphon (the first one was invented in 1813) with leafy decorations and the maker's name on it in a frosted-glass effect; or a Codd-stopper bottle – the top of the bottle is pinched in to hold a glass marble which was pressed tight against the mouth of the bottle by the gassy mineral-water inside (these were first made in 1872); or an old stoneware ginger-beer bottle.

You could have a lot of fun collecting tiny scent bottles, very decorative as a rule, whether old or new. Other 'minis' are salt pots, ink bottles, pill bottles and the tiny jars that hold spices, essences and herbs.

Rubbings are a way of making exact copies of certain things. You place a sheet of paper over the subject, rub black wax on, and you get a copy of what is under the paper. You can make rubbings of all sorts of things – for instance, some people collect coal-hole covers: these are the cast-iron discs you find in some city streets, over the holes through which coal used to be delivered to the house cellars under the pavement. You can take rubbings of the bark of different kinds of tree and make a collection of these. Anything which has a definite texture, or an engraved or embossed pattern (that is, a pattern standing up above the surface), can be the subject of a rubbing. To get the idea, put a coin under a piece of thin paper, rub a crayon to and fro on it, and hey presto!

You can even build up a picture by rubbing over different textures in turn – quite ordinary things like wire paper-clips, bits of netting, the ribbed edge of a dish, dried grasses (see page 46) – until you've got a sheet full of different textures placed so that they build up into a picture.

But the most spectacular rubbings of all are of the old brasses found in the floors of some churches, laid there as monuments to the knights and their ladies or other celebrities buried there centuries ago. They are usually depicted in all the splendour of their armour or their medieval wimples and veils. A life-size rubbing makes a very handsome picture to hang on your wall. When you have found a church with a brass you want to rub, ask the vicar's permission first. The polite way to do this is to write a letter, and to enclose with it a stamped envelope for his reply. Sometimes he may ask you to pay a fee for permission to rub.

Take a duster to clean the brass before you start, sheets of thin paper, like drawer-lining paper (buy this at a stationer's), Sellotape to hold it in place, and black wax crayon to do the rubbing – better still, buy some 'heelball' from an art shop.

When you have fastened the paper over the brass, start by marking on it the outline of the figure – feel it gently through the paper, and use your thumbnail to mark the outline. Then rub to and fro (starting with the head), being careful not to rub beyond the edges of the figure. Rub lightly and from side to side only.

When you have finished, you can get a smoother effect by rubbing over the blackened part with a soft rag.

To learn more about the history of brasses, and where to find them, read *Discovering Brasses and Brass Rubbing* (Cook, published by Shire) or *Brasses and Brass Rubbings* (Gittings, published by Blandford).

Some museums have collections of brass rubbings.

····⟫⟩≣ *BUTTONS* ≣⟨⟪····

Your mother and all her friends, and your friends' mothers, pretty certainly keep a button box, full of all sorts of odds and ends. If they know you're a keen button collector, who knows what treasures they might find for you?

Buttons – odd ones – can often be bought cheaply in sales at department stores, from street-market stalls, at jumble sales, and sometimes at jewellers' shops. In London, there is one shop that sells nothing but buttons – it's in St Christopher's Place off Wigmore Street and is called The Button Queen.

Buttons can be beautiful, buttons can be strange (some can be rare and costly too). Just think of all the materials used to make them: fabric, mother-of-pearl, leather, steel, plastic, wood, bone, brass, horn, glass – you could collect for years before you'd got one of every kind. Some people specialize – for example, collecting only buttons from uniforms (Army, Navy, etc, or railmen's – see page 100).

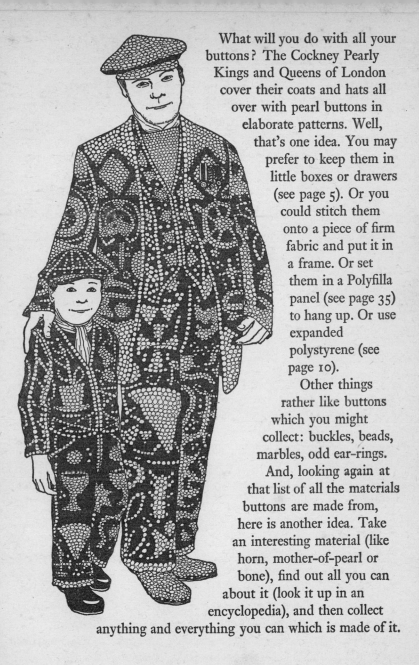

What will you do with all your buttons? The Cockney Pearly Kings and Queens of London cover their coats and hats all over with pearl buttons in elaborate patterns. Well, that's one idea. You may prefer to keep them in little boxes or drawers (see page 5). Or you could stitch them onto a piece of firm fabric and put it in a frame. Or set them in a Polyfilla panel (see page 35) to hang up. Or use expanded polystyrene (see page 10).

Other things rather like buttons which you might collect: buckles, beads, marbles, odd ear-rings. And, looking again at that list of all the materials buttons are made from, here is another idea. Take an interesting material (like horn, mother-of-pearl or bone), find out all you can about it (look it up in an encyclopedia), and then collect anything and everything you can which is made of it.

····✦══ CACTI ══✦····
(and other plants)

People who enjoy plants often have favourites which they start to collect, finding out all the different variations that exist within one plant family, and really getting to know the habits of that particular variety, how to propagate it, and so on. (Propagation means getting the plant to multiply so that from one specimen you get more and more plants each year.)

One kind of plant that makes a good collection is the cactus. You can find room for lots of little pots of them (or make a tray garden containing many). They don't cost much, last a long time, are easy to look after, and can produce brilliant, exotic flowers if they are given the right conditions – plenty of warmth and light. They hate damp, but they do need watering occasionally in summer (you can put a few drops of liquid fertilizer in the water to help them grow).

Some cacti produce offshoots – like tiny babies – which you can cut off and plant separately to grow up. You may need tweezers to handle the prickly ones. Another way to propagate cacti is to cut a tip off, leave it on one side until the cut has hardened, and then plant this. Or you can buy a packet of mixed cactus seeds and start from these – but it's a slow business.

You might like to make a beginning by finding the following half-dozen, which are sold by most garden shops and which have attractive flowers.

Gymnocalcium is a round, fleshy cactus with ribbed sides covered in clumps of sharp spikes. It produces just one or two flowers on top (red, yellow or white) but they're quite big.

Mammillaria is another dumpy one, with little rounded bumps all over it and a mass of prickles. It usually produces a pretty ring of tiny red flowers round the top.

Notocactus, another pincushion! Round, ribbed and with a fuzz of fine needles all over it. It produces just one or two big flowers at the top – red and yellow.

Opuntia is like a lot of pennies piled up edge to edge, usually with many prickles. Its flowers are red, yellow and orange.

Rebutia is like Mammillaria except that it grows in clumps and its many-coloured flowers stick out on stalks from the sides.

Christmas cactus is different from all the rest because it has stems that arch, and trail when they grow long, with red flowers that come out in winter. It needs a bit more watering than most, particularly in winter.

For ideas on other plants to collect, try my book *Growing Things* (published in Piccolo). A collection of plants grown from pips and fruit stones would be an original idea, described in this book.

A good book for beginners is *The Observer's Book of Cacti and Other Succulents* (Scott, Stanley and Henderson, published by Warne).

Collecting rare china is a serious and costly hobby, but fortunately there's lots of cheap, pretty china about on which you could make a start. Grown-up friends would probably be delighted to find a good home for odd pieces. Have you ever thought how decorative a panel of assorted teapot lids would be? (To make the panel, use Polyfilla as described on page 35.) Or you could collect saucers, or egg-cups, or mugs, or little bowls, or candlesticks, and arrange them on your mantelpiece or bookshelves. Another idea would be to collect pieces of china for their pattern; for instance, you could make a collection of flower patterns, patterns with birds and animals, Chinese patterns, and so on.

To hang plates on a wall, buy wire plate-hangers from a hardware shop, and some picture-pins.

As well as collecting cast-off pieces from friends and relations, you can pick up china – including china figures – very cheaply at sales in china shops and department stores, at jumble sales, or from junk stalls.

Strictly speaking, china means bone china or porcelain – very fine, thin, strong ware. You can just see your hand through it if you hold it up to the light. Most of what we have is really pottery (earthenware). As your collection builds up, you will notice other differences too. Very few things are hand-painted. Usually designs are printed on, or put on by transfers (and if you look closely you'll be able to see the joins between the bits of transfer). Some things have embossed patterns, or gilding.

Turn the saucer or bowl over and you should find the maker's name and symbol, and in time your collection might have in it pieces with names which were famous in the eighteenth and nineteenth centuries and still are today: Wedgwood, Worcester, Coalport, and so on. If you acquire older pieces, you may wonder just how old they are. Sometimes you can tell from the design of the symbol. On page 22, for instance, are three versions of the Worcester symbol. The first appears on china made between 1876 and 1891, the second after 1891 to about 1950, and the third has been used since then.

There are lots of books about china and china-marks – ask at your local library.

And when you're tired of collecting china, what about small glasses and glass bowls?

For free booklets on the history of china, write to the British Ceramic Manufacturers Federation, Station Road, Stoke-on-Trent, Staffordshire.

Who has never dreamed of treasure trove at the bottom of the garden? Coin collecting is the next best thing. It's not difficult to start with foreign coins, helped by friends who take holidays abroad. Try to collect coins from as many different countries as possible: you could pin up a map of the world and mark in each country as you add its coins to your collection. In addition, you may still come across some of the old pennies and halfpennies, sixpences and threepenny bits which were used before Britain went over to decimal coinage in 1971.

To collect old and rare coins is very expensive, but there are some kinds which you can buy from dealers at much lower prices (look up 'coin dealers' in the yellow pages of the phone book). There are even some Roman coins made of bronze which, being fairly plentiful, cost only pence – and how exciting to possess something made sixteen centuries ago, and bearing the head of a Roman emperor, minted (made) in London when this was occupied by the Romans. On the reverse side may be a picture commemorating a battle or recording some great new building: in those days, with no newspapers or television, the authorities often used coins to spread news of such events.

Because there happen to be lots of them that have survived, the silver pennies of Edward I are also obtainable at a fairly low cost: 20,000 of them were dug up in one hoard alone, in Staffordshire in 1831.

Not exactly coins, but nevertheless interesting to collect, are medieval jettons (counters used as a help when adding up accounts). So are tokens issued by tradesmen to their customers (particularly in the Midlands and North of England) as a kind of private coinage. There are still quite a lot of these about dating from the Civil War of the seventeenth century. In Victorian times, tradesmen and manufacturers often gave out decorative tokens advertising themselves, and these too would be interesting to collect if you like history. Hunt in junk shops, as well as going to specialist coin dealers.

You may think that, because our bank-notes of today represent more money than our coins, bank-notes would be dearer to collect. But some foreign notes, no longer valid for buying things, are very cheap indeed. They are colourful and decorative, and may have quite a lot of history expressed in their pictures and words. In Germany, in the significant year 1914, 56,000 different kinds of bank-note were issued! Even a French Revolution bank-note would not be ruinously expensive. So you see, there is immense scope for a collector. The bank-notes of Tsarist Russia are particularly splendid. Keep coins and bank-notes in transparent envelopes – you can make them yourself out of old plastic bags – or display them on trays lined with coloured paper.

There are plenty of books and magazines on coin collecting. You might start with *Discovering Coins* (Berry) and *Discovering Banknotes* (Lake – both published by Shire) or *Your Book of Coin Collecting* (Rayner, published by Faber).

This year, 1974, comic papers celebrate their centenary. And there is already a solemn Academy of Comic Book Arts in America! That's how serious collecting comics has become.

The very first comic strip appeared in an English magazine in 1847, and the first comic paper in 1874. You'd have quite a rarity for your collection if you came across one as old as that. The first great comic-paper hero was Ally Sloper (born 1884), and the first comic papers to become really famous were *Comic Cuts* and *Chips*: both ran from 1890 to 1953. Wearie Willie and Tired Tim were two tramps who appeared in *Chips* from its first issue to its last. *Puck* was an all-colour comic that began in 1904 and lasted until 1940; *The Rainbow* was another, famous for Tiger Tim. Mickey Mouse had his own comic in 1936; *Superman* (1938) and *Batman* (1940) also came from America. So these youthful heroes are really quite elderly now!

When *TV Comic* first appeared (1951) its cover star was Muffin the Mule, and there have been lots of other TV comics since then. New comics come and go all the time, so you won't be short of titles to add to your collection if you buy a different one each week.

But the real fun is hunting in attics and trunks and sheds to see if you can track down any old ones.

Read all about the old comics in *Discovering Comics* (Gifford, published by Shire).

Tarzan

by EDGAR RICE BURROUGHS

"WE ARE DOOMED," SOROS GROWLED. "I HAVE SEEN THE STRIPED DEATH ENTER THE ARENA WITH TEN MEN -----AND KILL THEM ALL!"

IMPULSIVELY, LURUL ROSE, STRIPPED HIS SHEATHED KNIFE FROM HIS BELT AND THREW IT TOWARD TARZAN.

AS THE WEAPON FELL AT HIS FEET, TARZAN CAST A FLEETING GLANCE TOWARD THE LOGES AND PICKED IT UP.

A traditional old craft has been revived in recent years: the making of corn dollies.

What are they? Originally they were straw figures woven from the very last sheaf of corn at harvest time. Once, people believed that the corn dolly was magic and would help to bring a good harvest the following year. Gradually, different places developed their own designs – the dollies turned into long twists (Essex), triangular decorations (Tewkesbury), crosses (Devon), and so on. Elaborate straw decorations were sometimes added to thatched roofs; or tiny ones were worn as buttonholes; or big ones were made for harvest festivals in churches.

The smaller ones are not expensive to buy, so you could start a collection. You could even learn how to make your own. You can get information about this from a firm called Art Straws Ltd (College Road, Fishponds, Bristol BS16) who make extra-long paper straws

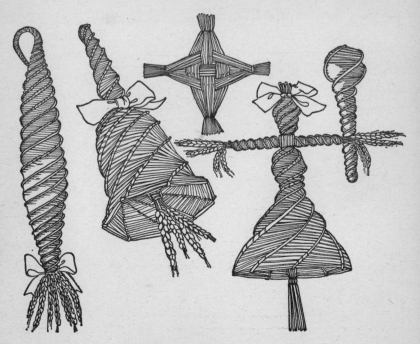

to use for this purpose if you can't get real straws. They also publish a 15p book of instructions.

Of course, other countries too had their own ways of weaving straw into figures and symbols: the Chinese like making straw fish. Things like this can be found in shops selling foreign crafts.

Another kind of figure you could collect is made from the dried outer leaves of maize.

By now you may be getting interested in what can be done with straw, dried leaves, rushes, reeds, cane, wicker and all the other materials like this, and you could start a wider collection with all kinds of things in it – little baskets, boxes, platters and many other woven objects.

A crystal may be so small that you can only see it with a microscope or it may be hundreds of feet high: at neither extreme would crystals be very collectable! But they are so fascinating (and decorative) that you might like to collect and study the more suitable ones.

Crystals are formed when the molecules of a substance join together to form a geometrical shape; the shape is always the same for a given substance, whatever the size of the crystal. Some are like cubes or pyramids, some more exotic in shape. With a magnifying glass you can study some crystals around the home – salt, for instance, or sugar.

You can make a crystal collection by – growing them! Just like a garden. You could build up a row of jam jars in your room, each containing a crystal 'plant'. (Keep them out of the reach of younger children!)

Alum is an easy one to start with. Buy it from a chemist. Into a jar, pour one fluid ounce of warm water (that's about 2 tablespoonfuls). Stir into it $1\frac{1}{2}$ teaspoonfuls of alum until it dissolves – a little should stay undissolved in the bottom, no matter how much you stir; add more, if need be, until this happens. This is called saturation.

Pour half into a saucer (don't pour in any undissolved alum), cover with kitchen foil and put aside for a few days – until all the water has gone and some tiny crystals are left. Choose four or five big enough for you to tie pieces of fine fuse-wire round, and lift them off. (If there are no separate crystals, but only a mass, you'll have to start again.) If the crystals are too small, add a drop of solution to each; when dry, add another – and another. These are called seed crystals.

To make big crystals, put $\frac{1}{2}$ pint warm water into a jar, stir in enough alum to saturate (about 2 ounces), cover the jar and leave it for a day, shaking it once or twice. Now pour this through a clean handkerchief into another jar. Tie a piece of wire round one of your seed crystals to hang it in the liquid and tie the other end through a hole in a cardboard disc which you can put over the jar like a loose lid. The seed crystal should hang freely in the middle of the liquid. It is important to leave the jar now in a cool place where the temperature does not go up or down. As the water slowly evaporates, the crystal will grow. It should be the size of a pea in a week and the size of a walnut after a month or two. Lengthen the thread as the water-level drops, and when it is down to one inch, top up with a fresh lot of alum-saturated water. Once you remove a crystal from liquid it is best protected from the air, so seal it in transparent plastic.

Other chemicals to use are as follows:

Potassium sodium tartrate (buy 12 ounces): colourless crystals.
Chromium potassium sulphate (8 ounces): rich purple crystals.
Copper sulphate (6 ounces): brilliant blue.
Nickel sulphate (12 ounces): blue-green.

And lots more: ask the chemist to advise you. Some probably in the house already are salt, borax and boric acid.

Hypo crystals are another of the 'instant' sort (photographic shops sell hypo). Heat, but don't boil, $\frac{1}{4}$ cup of water and dissolve 1 pound of hypo in it (keeping a grain or two back). Cover and leave for several hours till cool. Drop just one dry grain in, and all the liquid will instantly fill with feathery crystals. (If by any chance this doesn't work first time, reheat, strain and cool the liquid – but use an absolutely clean pan or jar.)

A fascinating book, with much more about crystals and other ways to grow them, is *Exploring Crystals* by James Berry (Collier-Macmillan). Or look in books about minerals.

COCK PHEASANT

JAY

PARTRIDGE

PARROT

TURKEY

Collecting feathers begins very easily – just by keeping an eye open whenever you are out for a walk. Even on city pavements you may pick up pigeon feathers, while other wild birds' feathers can be found in the garden or countryside, gulls' feathers on the beach, and duck or swan feathers in any park which has a duck pond or stream with ducks.

Ask at the fishmonger's or butcher's whether you can have feathers from chickens, ducks, turkeys, geese, pheasants, partridge, grouse, guinea-fowl, etc. If you live in or visit the country, friendly farmers or gamekeepers may give you some.

Then there are zoos, wildlife parks and bird gardens: you may find even more exotic or colourful ones on the ground there – from parrots, flamingos and peacocks. Ask friends who travel abroad to see what they can find for you, or perhaps you have an overseas pen-friend who could help. Some of your friends may keep parrots or other cage birds: or you may find a helpful petshop owner.

What are you going to do with your collection of feathers, which by now is getting quite big? Perhaps you're curious about the origin of some which you can't name. There are dozens of bird books you can consult. You already have some clues: you know where you found the feather (woodland, seaside, etc), you have some idea of the size of the bird from the length of the feather, you know something about its colouring. Your natural history or zoology teacher may be able to help you, or you could seek advice at a zoo or a natural history museum if you get stuck. You could fasten your feathers into a scrapbook (one page for each type of bird), writing on each one where you found it, the date, and the type of feather – wing, tail, etc.

You can, instead, just collect feathers because they're pretty (and make plain ones even prettier by dyeing them, or using a gold paint spray), putting them in a vase or making things with them – for instance, turn some into a picture of a bird with real feather body, tail and wings. You could hang up a cardboard bird with feather wings and tail; make a feather head-dress or mask for yourself; frame a round mirror with feathers sticking out all round from behind, like rays. Or, like the Wai-Wai Indians of South America, tie tiny bits among beads to make a fabulous necklace.

How birds use feathers is described in the *Piccolo Picture Book of Birds* by Robin Kerrod and John Rignall.

Wherever pine-trees grow, or spruces or larches, or any kind of fir, you will find cones on their branches or lying on the ground. They are the flowers produced by these trees. Sometimes their scales are shut up close. Later, when warm weather comes, they're wide open and they may have turned from green to brown. Look at how they are made and how each tiny scale is designed – with a bract at the back and (sometimes) a seed still visible at the base inside, perhaps with a little wing on it. A fir cone is an elaborate and fascinating thing!

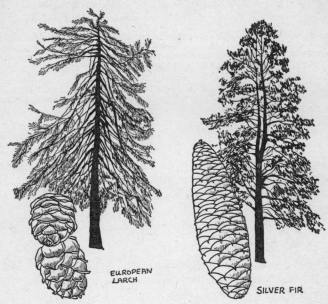

EUROPEAN
LARCH

SILVER FIR

Every type of fir has a different type of cone: in fact, on one tree you may find two kinds of cone, male and female. Sometimes one grows high on the tree and the other lower down; sometimes both are on the same branch, one at the tip and the other further along. Some cones stand up on top of the branches like candles, others hang down. Some grow to be six inches big, and others never more than one inch or less; some are slim and some are plump; some are smooth and neat, others loose and wavy.

Collect all the cones you can, keeping your eyes open on country walks and whenever you are in parks or gardens and, with the help of a tree book or of knowledgeable friends (like a teacher, park gardener, or curator in a natural history museum), label each one with its name, where you found it, and the date.

If you want to keep your cones in a permanent systematic display, you might like to do it my way. Take a box lid of suitable size, line it with a sheet of plastic film (old plastic bags will do), and pour into it half an inch of a thick mixture of Polyfilla – add very little water to the powder, just enough to make a dough that can be spread. Press a loop of wire or string into the middle of one edge (to hang the panel up later on). Now press the cones into the Polyfilla, leave overnight, and you will find they have set hard in place.

Of course, you can do lots of other things with fir cones like painting or gilding them, gluing them onto box lids or round tin lids for candlesticks, making little figures out of them, or even, if you have 'spares' from your collection, putting them on the fire to crackle and make a fragrant smell one winter's night.

A useful book for identifying fir cones and much else is *Trees and Bushes in Wood and Hedgerow* (Vedel and Lange, published by Methuen) or get *Know your Conifers* (Forestry Commission, published by Her Majesty's Stationery Office – HMSO).

STONE PINE

DOUGLAS FIR

FISH

Collecting live fish begins with buying a glass tank (unless you have a garden pond), or making one by tacking thick plastic sheeting (1,000 gauge) onto a wood frame. Or you could make do with a plastic washing-up bowl. It is easier to collect fish that like cool water: tanks for tropical fish have to be heated. The tank needs to be kept out of sunlight or other heat, yet with enough light for the plants to grow.

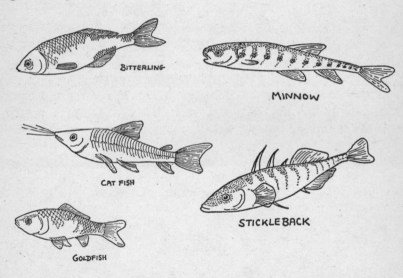

BITTERLING

MINNOW

CAT FISH

STICKLEBACK

GOLDFISH

Petshops sell aquarium compost or gravel (you'll need enough for a two-inch layer all over the bottom of the tank) and water plants to put in: they have unusual names like Fairy Moss, Frogbit and Mare's Tail. Add a few little rocks or pebbles, too. Finally, fill gently with water, and put a sheet of transparent plastic over the top to keep dust out. The only other thing you need to get is fish food; live daphnia, a kind of shrimp (from a petshop) are excellent, or you can breed white worms in a box of earth (feeding them bread and milk). Some fish will eat raw fish or even cat-food.

The first fish for your collection is likely to be a goldfish, and there are plenty of different types to choose from. The glowing colours of the stickleback may attract you, but he needs his own tank because he attacks other fish. Minnows are less aggressive, and sometimes just as colourful. Some fish which grow too big later are well worth keeping in an indoor tank while young: carp, tench, orfe, rudd. The gudgeon, stone loach, American catfish, perch, ruffe and bull-head are also suited to tanks. Or you could keep small eels. Many of these can be caught in streams and ponds, but if you are not near either, get them from a petshop.

As well as fish, obtain some water snails – they help to keep the water clear. There is quite a variety of them to choose from, too: you might even decide to collect snails instead of fish.

If you haven't much space, you could try a different kind of water collection and create a miniature aquarium in a jam jar, with small freshwater shrimps, water insects like caddis-worms and water-boatmen, and the tiniest of water-plants, such as duckweed.

Anyone living by the sea might decide to make a marine aquarium, but this is more complicated as you have to aerate the water to make it like the sea with its waves endlessly in motion.

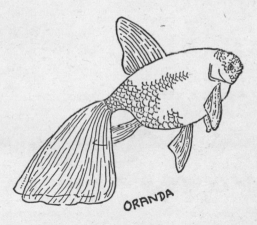

ORANDA

There are plenty of books to choose from: a good one about keeping fish, covering all types, is *Life in the Aquarium* by Philip Barker (Bell). To learn about our own pond and stream creatures, try *Pond Life* (Chadwick, published in Puffin) or, more advanced, *Pond and Stream Life of Europe* (Barth, published by Blandford).

An array of flags of all nations, hung from strings across your room, would be a very colourful collection. Or you could make small ones, fix a large world map on the wall, and pin them in place.

You can look them up in an encyclopedia at school, at home or in a library. Since most of them are made up of stripes, they aren't difficult to create. Buy a pack of assorted, coloured papers; cut them out and stick them onto sheets of plain paper.

You will soon do all the big countries' flags. The fun begins when you try to track down little countries, and get your friends guessing which is which.

CEYLON   CANADA   BRAZIL

ALBANIA   ALGERIA   BARBADOS

SOUTH KOREA   LEBANON   ISRAEL

MAURITANIA   PAKISTAN   SINGAPORE

The flags on page 38 are only a few: I've chosen ones that have rather more unusual designs than just stripes. To copy them, you will need to pencil the emblems onto paper and paint them.

Here's how to copy a flag – enlarging it.

Choose your flag, divide it in four, then into sixteen.

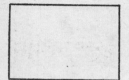 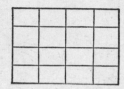 

Take a larger sheet of paper, divide into sixteen, then copy.

There are lots of other kinds of flags to collect. Ships signal with them; the Queen has the Royal Standard and her own personal flag, too; there are flags for different organizations – like the Scouts, the Red Cross, the Olympic Games. Souvenir shops often sell pennants – triangular flags – with the coat-of-arms of a town on them, and you could collect these to string up in your room. And then you can call yourself a vexillologist – an expert on flags.

Read the *Piccolo Picture Book of Flags* (Pitt and Ralphs).

It's fun to pick wild flowers in summer – in the countryside, or on commons and wasteground – but never take any that you suspect might be uncommon. Yours might be the last ones in that particular place, and by picking the flower and seed heads, you could rob the area of the plant for ever.

That still leaves plenty which grow abundantly and which you can take, but as wild flowers soon wilt there is not much point in just putting them in a vase. You can instead build up a permanent collection by pressing them. Choose flat flowers that will press smoothly. Either lay each flower on a piece of paper and put transparent self-adhesive plastic over (this must be done immediately after picking); or else press the flowers between the pages of a book until they are dry, which may take a week, then glue them onto paper. While they are drying, put the book under something heavy, like a pile of other books. Or you could put them between newspapers under a doormat. Don't use any glossy paper or they will stick to it.

You could, if you prefer, make a collection of garden flowers instead.

Look each flower up in a flower book – there are plenty to choose from – and write its name against it. As many flowers are similar, it helps if you have also one or two of its leaves to help identify it. Other clues will be where you found it and in what month, so write these down too.

You could also make a collection of ferns like this – in Britain alone there are 40 species to go hunting for. Mosses and lichens are other kinds of plants which could form a collection. These can't be pressed, so you would need to keep each one in an envelope or matchbox.

There are a number of books about ferns and mosses to help you identify them.

If, like me, you prefer to do something decorative with your collection of dried plants, here are some ideas. Find an old picture frame and cut a piece of deep-coloured felt or blotting-paper to fit it. Then make a flower picture. You could either glue the dried flowers and leaves on, to look like a nosegay or spray; or you could remove all stalks and make them into a decorative pattern. You might like to paint a picture of a basket and fill it with dried flowers, or create a garden picture with them. You could use dried flowers to make Christmas or birthday cards.

I use dried mosses, lichens and ferns together with twigs and pebbles to make little scenes or still-lifes, pressed into a base of clay or other modelling material.

A set of two books I've written might be useful to you:

My Flower Book is designed to hold a wild-flower collection, with colour pictures on one side and spaces to glue the actual flower in on the other side. *Fun and Flowers* contains ideas for things to make and do with flowers (both books from Galt's toyshops). If you want to know more about flowers, get *The Clue Book of Flowers* (Allen and Denslow, published by Oxford University Press).

Spoor is the word for the footprints animals leave behind. If you live in the country you could 'collect' these prints by making plaster casts, which is quite easy, and then identifying them from books when you get home.

You need to go out with the following things: plastic bags (tightly fastened) containing some Plaster-of-Paris powder or Polyfilla, a bottle of water, and some kitchen foil. When you find a spoor, brush away any twigs, etc, make an inch-deep ring from several thicknesses of foil and stand it round the spoor so that it follows the outline. Pour some water into one of the bags of powder, squeezing it a lot to make sure it's thoroughly mixed – it should be like cream – before pouring it into the ring. Wait until it has set hard before removing the foil and turning the cast over.

What sort of spoor might you find? Hedgehog – a line of tiny tracks left during the previous night. Rabbit – as it hops along, it leaves its prints in fours; forepaws close together, then hind legs. Adder: a wriggly trail. Crow – three fore-toes close together, a long hind-toe, and scratchmarks between each footprint. Badger – bear-like foot-pads with five long claws. Shelduck – webbed feet striding along, turned slightly inwards.

You can study pictures of these and many more in *Tracks* (Ennion and Tinbergen, published by Oxford University Press).

FOSSILS

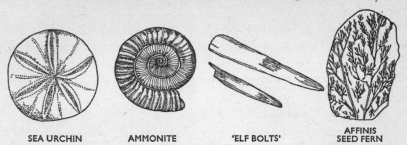

SEA URCHIN   **AMMONITE**   **'ELF BOLTS'**   **AFFINIS SEED FERN**

Fossils are the remains of animals and plants embedded in rock. They can be millions of years old. The existence of dinosaurs is known only because their footprints or skeletons have turned up in various places, petrified in rock. You are not very likely to find anything as exciting as this, but you could easily build up a collection of fossilized shells, ferns, insects, etc.

You need to know a bit about rocks (see page 88), for fossils do not occur in all kinds of rock. They are never found in granite, for instance, so it's a waste of time looking in a granite district. Areas of limestone, chalk, clay or shale will be more rewarding – so the first move is a visit to your local library to ask for a geological map of your area, which will indicate what the possibilities are. Then look at another map, a one-inch-to-the-mile Ordnance Survey, to see whereabouts in the right districts there are cliffs, public beaches and quarries, and off you go (wearing old clothes, for fossil-hunting can be dirty work). You might find fossils on the banks of streams or roads. You will need hammer and chisel.

If you go to a quarry, you *must* ask the foreman's permission to enter, and if he tells you any part of the quarry is dangerous, don't go near it – rocks might fall on you, or the ground give way.

When you spot a fossil, place the chisel edge on the rock just above it and hit this with the hammer. Try to knock off a piece of rock a little bigger than the fossil itself. You may find fossils among the loose rocks on the quarry floor.

There are plenty of books on rocks and fossils to help you: see page 89. You could also read *Mary Anning's Treasure* by Helen Bush (published by Gollancz), a fascinating true story about a girl who collected fossils and discovered actual dinosaur bones.

Here's a kind of collecting that can help other people in need: the sick or poor or disabled. Lots of 'good causes' welcome things that most families regard as rubbish, because if they get enough of them, they know where to sell them to raise funds, or how to put them to good use.

When you have collected from all your friends a big pile of what's needed, send it off – and, if you are interested enough, ask the organization concerned to tell you a little about the work it does. Some have leaflets.

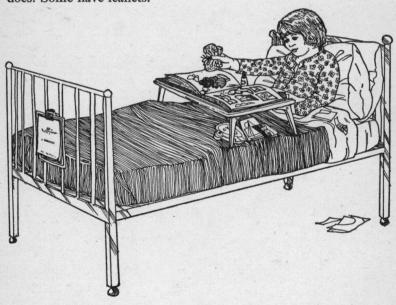

What to collect and where to send it

Milk-bottle tops and other silver foil things (*not* silver paper from cigarette packets):
Guide Dogs for the Blind Association, 113 Uxbridge Road, London W5. (If you collect 28 pounds or more, local National Carriers will collect it from you.)
Knitting-wool leftovers:
Women's Royal Voluntary Service (any local branch).

Old sheets:
 Toc H Women's Association (contact your local branch).
Old shoes and clothes:
 Oxfam (any local branch).
Any saleable articles:
 Help the Aged, 8 Denman Street, London W1, and local
 branches.
Toys, dolls and games:
 Barnardo's. (Gifts in Kind, Woodford Bridge, Essex – send a
 postcard asking for the address in your area where you should
 send or take your gifts.) Or send them to any local Children's
 Home.
Books (for sending to poor countries):
 Ranfurly Library, Kensington Palace Barracks, Kensington
 Church Street, London, W8 (children's books most welcome).
Old Christmas and Birthday cards, or postcards:
 Local hospitals or nurseries may like them, for children to make
 scrapbooks.
Stamps (British as well as foreign):
 British Cancer Research Campaign, 2 Carlton House Terrace,
 London SW1; or Shelter (any local branch).
Magazines:
 Seafarers Education Service, 207 Balham High Road, London
 SW17 (or any local hospital).
Playing cards and games:
 Women's Royal Voluntary Service (local branch).
Trading Stamps:
 Save the Children Fund, 29 Queen Anne's Gate, London SW1
 (or local branch).
Old jewellery, silver, buttons, etc:
 Children's Society, 50 Claremont Road, Bristol 7.
Old blankets and clothes:
 Lambeth Mission, Lambeth Road, London SE1 (or Salvation
 Army – local office).
The 'Blue Peter' television programme collects the following
 things: wool and cotton fabrics, old model cars, bits of brass, old
 cutlery, jewellery, watches, coins – anything metal. Its address
 is: Television Centre, London W12.

Grass isn't 'just grass': it's a whole world of plants, each with roots, stalk, leaves and flowers just like any other. Even in an ordinary lawn there is likely to be a variety of different grasses mixed up. Grass (which includes grains like wheat and rice that feed people the world over) is vital to the existence of animals and of us. Except where vegetation has been driven out and only deserts remain, or where ice covers the ground permanently, grass grows pretty well everywhere.

So wild grasses can make an interesting and important subject for a collection. Keep your specimens in a special scrapbook. Press, dry and glue just like wild flowers (see page 40). Look up their names in books in order to identify them and find out more about them: most wild-flower books include grasses.

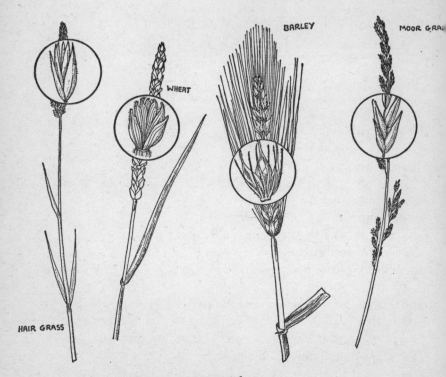

BARLEY

MOOR GRAS

WHEAT

HAIR GRASS

Use a magnifying glass to study them. Their small flowers lack scent and colour, but some have fascinating shapes – you may like to draw them (or make rubbings – see page 16), and then make decorative patterns and pictures of them. The best time of year to collect is summer, when the grasses produce their flowers. But you can find dried-up grasses at any time of year: these are very decorative when arranged in a vase or pushed into a lump of Plasticine or other modelling material.

Apart from wild grasses, you could make a collection of cultivated grains – looking for new ones whenever you go for a walk or car-ride in the country. Wheat, barley, oats, rye and maize (sweetcorn) are the ones you're most likely to find. Look on a bag of flour for the name and address of the miller who made it, and write to him to ask if he can send you any 'ears' of wheat from other countries. Then you can compare them with the home-grown wheat already in your collection and see how they differ. He may also be able to send you booklets about the story of wheat. The manufacturer of your breakfast porridge might help you similarly with oats; or a brewer of beer with barley. Kelloggs (Box 278, Stretford, Manchester) will send you nutritional information about grains. Look each grain up in an encyclopedia – you could then make a map showing whereabouts in the world they are grown, and do drawings of all the food products that are made from them. Perhaps you could visit a flour mill or a brewery and actually see the grains being used.

If you collect grains from fields, take them only from the edge. Never walk into a field with crops growing, and always close gates behind you in case animals get in and damage the crops. From straw left behind in the field after harvest, you could make corn dollies (see page 28).

Apart from using reference books to identify grasses, you may enjoy reading *World Provider: The Story of Grass* (Riedman, published by Abelard-Schuman).

In the days when things were delivered by horse-and-cart, the horses often presented a dazzling sight wearing brasses on their leather harness. The genuine old ones are now regarded as antiques and they cost quite a lot, but there are modern copies which you can buy more cheaply. They're not only decorative but have some interesting stories attached to them. Try gift shops, department stores, junk shops, even Woolworth's.

Originally, in the eighteenth century, brasses were worn as charms to ward off the 'evil eye' and often had a design based on the sun. The designs on others varied. Farm horses often wore brasses with ploughs or wheatsheafs on them. Some carried the crest of the landlord who owned them. Often brasses commemorated great events (such as a coronation or a victory) or famous men: modern brasses not only copy these but sometimes portray famous men of modern times, like Churchill or Montgomery. Horses which worked on the railways often had an engine on their brasses, those from the docks a ship or an anchor, while brewers' horses might carry a barrel emblem.

If you are keen on horses, you might add to your collection of brasses lots of other things too and make yourself *a horse museum*. It could contain horseshoes, model horses, newspaper cuttings about horses, books on horses, autographs of Olympic riders, coins or stamps with horses on them, photos of horsey inn signs (see page 50), horse legends, old prints with horses (see page 84) and so on.

Perhaps you could get an old bookcase for your display, putting labels against each item, just as they do in real museums. Alternatively, use short shelves of thick card with a hole pierced at each corner, to hang up on cords and picture pins (picture pins, sold by hardware shops, do not harm the walls as nails would).

A home museum like this could be made up on any subject that interests you.

If you prefer, you could collect brass objects of all kinds, particularly small things. Thimbles used often to be made of brass; you may come across brass boxes or other trinkets from India, elaborate decorated; there are lots of brass candlesticks about; and what about old fire irons – pokers, hearth brushes, toasting forks, trivets for the kettle, and bellows? A whole collection could be made of little brass bells, or of doorknockers, or of weights, or of wall-plaques in brass – new or old. Inkstands turn up cheaply in junk shops because so few people use old-fashioned pens now. Can you find any interesting designs of nutcrackers? Pipe-stoppers are little brass pushers to press tobacco down in a pipe: they were, and still are, made in fanciful shapes such as characters from Dickens's stories.

These make an interesting subject if you like drawing or are good with a camera.

As long ago as Roman times, inns carried a sign – a bunch of vine-leaves – to tell people who couldn't read that here was a place where wine could be had. Decorative signs were common in the fifteenth century and became so elaborate in the seventeenth century (sometimes stretching right across the street) that Charles II decreed that they must be reduced in size. There are still plenty of fanciful, strange, gaudy or historic ones to be seen today, and many tell an interesting story.

You could start a scrapbook of inn signs. Under each drawing or photograph, you should write the name and address of the inn and the date when you spotted it. With your parents' help in talking to the publican (the man who runs the inn), you may learn how the inn got

its name and how old it is, and you could write this down, too. Your collection could specialize, selecting only royal or heraldic signs, say, or animal ones, or travel ones (ships, rail, coach, etc), signs to do with trades (like 'The Mason's Arms', or 'Three Horseshoes' – for a smithy), sports, or historic events and people.

Another way to mount a collection of inn signs would be to make really big paintings of each one, then put them all round your room. If you like, you could first put up a length of lining paper (across not down the wall), bought from a wallpaper shop, fastening it to the wall with Blu-Tack or double-sided Sellotape which, when removed later, leaves no mark. Then glue the inn signs along this.

Lots of inns are called 'Crown' or 'King's Head' because inn-keepers of long ago wanted to keep in with the royalist parties, and for the same reason royal emblems like the rose, the white boar (Richard III), the white hart (Richard II), the red dragon (Henry VII) and the oak (Charles II) were often used. A red lion was the crest of John of Gaunt, a white bear that of the Earls of Kent, a swan that of the Dukes of Buckingham, a white horse that of the Earls of Arundel – and so on. Signs like these are a clue that the inn may have some connection with a king or noble famous in history.

As for animal signs, a bear or cock *may* indicate that at one time bear-baiting or cock-fighting took place at the inn; fox or hounds that the local hunt used to start from there (and may still do so). Lots of pubs are called 'Bird in Hand', referring to the ancient sport of falconry. Cats often turn up – there are even inns called 'Cat and Fiddle', 'Puss in Boots' and 'Whittington and Cat'.

There are plenty of books about historic inns. A good one to begin with is *Discovering Inn Signs* (Lamb and Wright, published by Shire) and there is also *Introduction to Inn Signs* (Delderfield, published by Pan).

····❧❧ ═ *INSECTS* ═ ❧❧····

Here is a whole new world of life to discover! At least 20,000 different kinds of insect exist. Some are unpopular (gardeners hate greenflies, housewives kill ants) but they have extremely interesting habits to study, and because they come in such a variety of weird shapes and colours they make an exciting collection. You will need a magnifier to see the smallest ones clearly. The best time to start is summer, but you can go on collecting insects in winter: they will be hidden away hibernating and may look dead, though they are not.

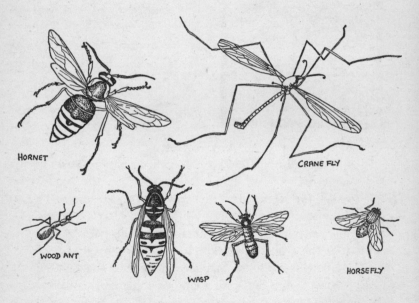

HORNET

CRANE FLY

WOOD ANT

WASP

HORSEFLY

Go hunting in gardens or parks (look for traces like blotches or holes in leaves which tell you where insects have been), in corners of sheds, under stones, in cellars or attics, around tree trunks or posts, among dead leaves. Around the house you might find silver-fish or house-flies or the grubs of the clothes moth. From petshops you can buy silkworm eggs to rear on lettuce leaves later.

Spiders aren't true insects, nor are worms, centipedes, millipedes and woodlice, but there's no reason why you shouldn't collect these too, if you like. Caterpillars and larvae are the young of certain insects, waiting to turn into moths, beetles, etc. True insects are those which have six legs, a pair of feelers, and a body divided into three parts: head, thorax and abdomen.

You could have a live collection of insects, or you could mount on cardboard a collection of dead ones. I like watching live insects: even worms are interesting in a big glass jar half full of earth and topped with decaying leaves – they make elaborate tunnels which you can see through the glass (but keep the light out most of the time).

The silkworms mentioned above are very interesting to watch. The young caterpillars repeatedly cast off their skins. When they are two or three inches long, if you tie some straw into bundles and make them arch over the caterpillars' box, they will go up it and start spinning silk until each has made itself a cocoon. Inside this, the worm turns into a chrysalis (you can open one and look) and about two or three weeks later a silkworm moth emerges.

You can collect other caterpillars (or chrysalids) and keep them until they turn into butterflies or moths. Chrysalids are most likely to be in cracks of the bark on trees or at the foot of trees. Keep them cool.

The other way to collect is to kill the insects first. This is done by preparing a screwtop jar with lethal fumes in it. Either get some laurel leaves, crush them, put them in, and cover them with a disc of paper; or buy from a chemist a little ethyl acetate and pour this onto a small sponge or cottonwool pad in the bottom of the jar. *Don't breathe these fumes in yourself.* Drop the insects in, screw the lid on, and wait until they are dead. Then you can fix them with delicate dabs of glue, looking up their names in insect books to write beside them. Such books will also tell you how to catch the elusive ones.

It is a pity to kill insects that are helpful to man, or decorative. The ladybird (red with black spots) is both, and so are bees. Some butterflies and moths have destructive grubs, yet, because butterflies are beautiful and are becoming rare, it would be a shame to kill these for a collection.

A third way, therefore, to 'collect' is to keep an insect diary. Under each date, write down each insect you find, where it was, and what it was doing. Or have another book with blank pages, and whenever you find an insect, write its name at the top of the page, draw it (then let it go), and write down everything you can find out about its habits. You could buy some sticky-paper stars (or dots), and if the insect is a friend of man put a gold or red star on its page; if an enemy, a black one.

There are lots of other angles to insect-collecting. You could go in for water insects if you have a pond or stream nearby (see page 37). Or specialize in the insects associated with trees: you might collect galls (oak apples) and study the insects that make these, or find out about the insect life of an apple orchard. Or try keeping foreign insects: petshops sell African stick insects which look just like (you'd never guess) sticks.

There are plenty of books on insects. Good ones are *The Clue Book of Insects* (Allen and Denslow, published by Oxford University Press), *The Insect World* (Manning, published by World's Work), *Insects in Colour* (edited by Riley and published by Blandford) and, covering more than insects, *The Naturalist's Handbook* (Geoffrey Watson, published in Piccolo) and *A Zoo on Your Window Ledge* (Spoczynska, published by Muller). *Very Small Animals* (in the 'Starters Activities' series published by Macdonald) is about keeping live insects. You can learn more about insects – and get help in identifying specimens – by visiting zoos and natural history museums.

Facts are things you acquire all day and every day, but you might like to make a special collection of odd, interesting, useful or strange information.

Take names, for instance – of people or places. Most of them have interesting origins or meanings, which you can find out from books. You could write down the names of every person you meet or place you go to, then, bit by bit, track down their meanings.

Or you could take a topic and find out every odd thing you can; each time you acquire a scrap of information you could add it to your notebook. And illustrate some of them.

I started collecting facts about – eggs! Here are some of the things I 'bagged':

In every egg, there's a little airspace: the smaller it is, the fresher the egg.

English people prefer brown eggs, but Americans prefer white ones.

Most people eat five eggs a week.

The biggest egg laid by a hen weighed one pound.

By whisking an egg-white hard, you can fluff it up to SIX times its original size.

Twelve eggs give you about $1\frac{1}{4}$ pounds of food, more nourishing than meat.

The original word for egg was *ey*. That's why eagles' nests (their 'eggeries') are called eyries.

The dearest egg in the world was worth over £2,000. It was made with gold and diamonds for a Czar of Russia.

The Guinness Book of Records (edited by N. D. McWhirter and R. McWhirter) is full of strange facts. The same people who compiled this have done other books with curious information in them, such as *Surprising Facts about Plants*.

Other people's throw-outs may contain treasures for you! And other chapters in this book tell how many things once thrown on the rubbish heap are now greatly prized and sometimes bought and sold for big sums: old newspapers, postcards, tickets and tins. What other kinds of things may be worth saving from a sad death in the dustbin? Here are three ideas – I'm sure you can think of more.

Broken clocks and radios. Collect as many as you can. Take them to pieces – carefully (that way you'll learn a lot about how they work). Maybe you could even repair some (there are books on how to do it). Sort the pieces, then use them to make decorative objects. Necklaces, for instance, or a montage picture, like the one opposite.

Plastic pots. When you've got enough you can make these into models or figures (they make fine robots, especially squeezy-bottles). Decorate a collection of cream and yogurt pots and use them to plant your cactus collection in (see page 20). The best way is to cover them in felt or coloured paper, then glue or braid, beads or other trimmings. Because of their shape, cutting out the cover needs a special pattern, so instructions for this are given on the last page of the book.

Lace. When your mother or her friends have nighties or slips they're going to throw out, ask for any lace trimmings. Cut one-foot lengths and glue into a scrapbook which has dark-coloured pages. Get a history of lace from the library, and write out the story of lace to add to your sample-book.

Then there are junk shops, stalls and jumble sales where other people's 'rubbish' can be bought for a few pence. Do you know that these days there are serious collectors who spend a lot of money on things like old fountain-pens, money-boxes, pincushions, walking-sticks, spring tape-measures, or thimbles? I've yet to hear of any-one collecting broken cigarette lighters – but there's almost nothing under the sun that somebody, somewhere, doesn't collect! Even museums now often display collections of old tools, or even of old kitchen utensils and things like irons.

Here's an idea for you: tiny spoons, the sort used with coffee cups, or for salt and mustard. Often they have quite decorative handles, and are made in all kinds of materials as well as silver: painted china, boxwood, carved bone, plastic, glass. Or you could make a collection of small boxes. Or of paper-weights. Or of treen. (What's that? an old word for little things made out of trees – just wood!) What about nutcrackers, inkwells, or knobs and knockers? Or fans? Or old tiles, table mats or ashtrays?

Even the bits of rubbish found when tidying drawers may have their uses. The 'junk lady' in the picture is made from broken paperclips, pencil-shavings, card, silver paper, string, etc.

Here's a collection you can start at once, by a quick sortie in the kitchen larder (with permission, of course), adding continually whenever your mother goes shopping. And the help of your friends' mothers might be enlisted too. It's an idea shown to me by my young friend Bobo, who's on the cover of this book.

Buy or make a scrapbook with big pages. A looseleaf one is best. At the top of each page write the name of a country. Then glue on to the page labels taken from cans or packets of food from the country concerned. This will make a very colourful scrapbook in the end, and you may be surprised to discover how many of the foods we eat come from far places.

Later you could draw or buy a big map of the world to fix on the wall. Then stick a map-pin (the kind that has a big, coloured head) in each country, with a coloured thread tied to it. Take the other end of the thread right across to the edge of the map and fix it to another pin, through a card on which you have written (or drawn) all the foodstuffs in your label-book which come from that country. This is an entertaining way of learning geography, and the produce of different areas!

Or you could do the same with foods from Britain (Cheshire cheese, Devonshire cream, Scotch beef and so on). Or you could make a collection of cheese labels only.

To return to your 'world' scrapbook, just look, for instance, at what it might have on the page headed 'Spain': luscious pictures of apricots and peaches, the pretty tissue paper a Spanish orange was wrapped in, a sardine-can wrapper with a picture of a fishing-boat, a splendid gold label from a bottle of sherry, or some showing rich, red tomatoes and pimentos, a wine label with a picture of a donkey carrying a basket of grapes.

If you enjoy cookery, you might like to add to your scrapbook recipes from each country, using the foodstuffs you've collected. And if by now you've got really interested in the subject, you could get information about how the different foods are grown or pro-cessed, and put this in too. There are quite a lot of organizations who will send you this information free (and recipes) if you write to them (see pages 110–11). When you go on a holiday abroad one day, you can look out for the crops of these foods growing in the fields and imagine how, later on, you may eat the very same crop out of a can or packet at home.

There are, of course, lots of other kinds of label collections you can make – not just foreign ones and not just foods. Pick any topic that interests you. I once saw an old chest-of-drawers entirely covered in pictures of flowers from seed-packets: there's another good idea for making a label collection.

Sources of information about how foods are produced (free unless otherwise stated) are listed on page 110–11.

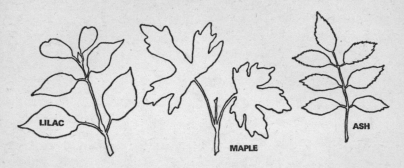

LILAC

MAPLE

ASH

Leaves of trees (or, if you prefer, of plants) make a good collection because they're easy to get in town or country, have such a lot of variety, and don't take up much space. You could combine them with collecting other tree things: bark rubbings (see page 16), fir cones (see page 34), seeds and nuts (see page 92) and even treen (see page 57).

Leaves can be pressed just like flowers (see page 40) so that you can keep them in a scrapbook, writing down their names and also when and where you found each one; or you can make them into pictures. When dry they can be painted or gilded, used decoratively on boxes or lampshades, given wire stems to make into decorations, and so on. Provided they are not too young when you pick them, branches of leaves can be made to last by standing them in a jar containing equal quantities of glycerine and water (in a cool, dim place) until they have soaked it all up.

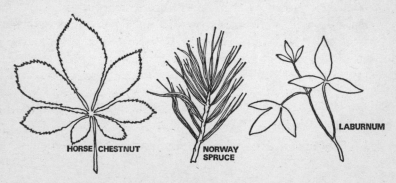

HORSE CHESTNUT

NORWAY SPRUCE

LABURNUM

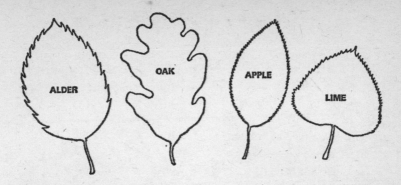

Apart from their shapes and colours (particularly those lovely autumn colours), the leaves of trees are full of interest – some downy and some shiny, some that tremble and flicker in the breeze, some sticky, others rough as sandpaper. Find out whether there is in your neighbourhood a botanical garden or an arboretum (that is, a wood consisting of specially planted trees chosen for their variety or rarity) and go leaf-hunting there.

You could make a separate collection of skeleton leaves: leathery leaves from which all but a fine skeleton of veins has rotted away, leaving only a lacy outline. Though you can occasionally find these in woods and can buy artifically prepared ones at garden shops or florists, making them yourself is half the fun. Half fill a saucepan with water and put in one or two dessertspoons of soda. Heat it until it is nearly boiling, then put a leaf in to simmer gently for an hour. Cool, take it out and brush the softened flesh away with a nail-brush (if it won't come away, simmer a little longer). Now put it in bleach for an hour, then in a dish under a cold tap and let this dribble over it. You will now have your skeleton leaf.

Another way to collect leaves is by collecting living woodland plants – small ferns in particular. First get a glass tank (with a sheet of glass for a lid) or a big transparent plastic box: garden shops sell them. Buy some charcoal chips to put in the bottom, then a layer of peat, then one of compost (all sold by garden shops). Now you can plant the little ferns inside and put the lid on. Keep this in a cool place away from sunlight. You need never water it if the lid is kept on, except when adding a new fern to your collection.

Here's one for anybody who enjoys books and reading, and likes a good story. First, pick a suitable subject that appeals to you. Are you interested in a place (it might be Scotland), a mystery subject (like ghostly horsemen), birds (perhaps swans), adventure stories (maybe of ships and the sea), the saints, or plants (wild or garden ones)? Choose a topic and from now on go looking for myths and legends associated with it. Search books in the library (including poetry), ask friends what they know, when you visit old buildings, churches or ruins look out for strange carvings or pictures to do with your chosen subject – which you can photograph or draw. When you have filled a scrapbook with all your finds, you will almost have written a book on the subject – who knows, perhaps one day you *will* write a book about it!

Just to give you an idea, here is what I found when I started to collect *owl* stories. First I came across a Russian folk-tale about a hunter who was enticed across a river by a beautiful woman, but she turned into an owl before he could swim over and left him to drown in the icy flood. Next was a Greek myth about a king's child who was lost, and a mysterious owl surrounded by a swarm of bees led the searchers to an urn of honey in which the child had drowned. Also from ancient Greece I learnt about a strange dance in which men dressed up as owls and had to catch a small bird. The one I liked best is about Persephone who had been taken away to the Underworld but was released on condition that she ate nothing till she was back on earth. Alas, she did eat seven pomegranate seeds – in November – and one of the Underworld gardeners told tales. His name was Ascalaphus, and that is the Latin name of the Short-eared Owl, a bird prone to be particularly noisy in November, as you may have noticed if you live near woods.

Legends like these make very good subjects for drawings, so why not illustrate your book?

Or you could collect fabulous monsters. Churches are a good place to look for these, in carvings and so forth. You might find Dragons, symbols of evil – often trodden underfoot by St George or by knights on tombs or brasses (see page 16). The amphisbaena is a serpent with wings and a head at both ends – like Mr Facing-Both-Ways in *Pilgrim's Progress*. The Salamander, a winged dragon, lives in flames; the Basilisk is a serpent whose glance kills; the Griffin, half eagle and half lion, is a good beast; the Phoenix is a bird who rises from the ashes; and the Unicorn stands for purity and holiness. There are plenty of legends to be collected about all these.

What about making a little book of Christmas legends and customs, and giving it to your parents for a Christmas present?

If you want to make models or pictures of legendary creatures you may find another book of mine useful, *Make Your Own Monster* (Piccolo).

ou think the ABC is kid's stuff? Well, there's more to letters than you may think! – as the page opposite shows. Just look at all these different ways of printing the same letter.

The letters we use are thousands of years old, and in each century new designs have been created, some of them very decorative. Before printing was invented, the monks who wrote out manuscripts by hand often started each page with an involved decoration surrounding the first letter on it – like the Y that starts this page, but even more elaborate, coloured and gilded.

The people who choose what kind of lettering to use in books are called typographers. Look closely and you will see there are slight differences between the letters in one book and another. Each kind of type has its own name. For instance, this book is printed in Ehrhardt. Ordinary upright type is called Roman, *but the second part of this sentence is in italic – similar type but slanting*. Most letters have little lines (serifs) at top and bottom, but when they do not (as in the second part of this sentence) they are called 'sans serif'. Already you are learning about typography – and you can find out a lot more by borrowing from the library a book on the subject.

Now, if you find all this interesting, why not collect unusual letters and make your own book of type? A 26-page scrapbook will give you one page for each letter of the alphabet – but you will find more E's, S's and M's, for instance, than Q's, X's and Z's.

Cut the letters from magazines, newspapers, advertisements, labels, Christmas or birthday cards – there are plenty of hunting-grounds. Trace unusual, old letters out of old books.

You will soon want to start designing some letters of your own. Do your own initials and put them in your books and other posses-sions. Do your friends' initials to put on birthday cards or presents like bookmarks, little boxes, etc.

It's fun to find out about the place where you live. If you're ambitious, you could try to collect information about the history of the whole town or village. But it can be quite interesting to concentrate on just your own road and, of course, your own house in particular. Not many of us are lucky enough to live in very old, historic houses or streets, but even quite recent ones may have a story to tell. What, for instance, was there before the road was built?

You will be greatly helped by your public library. Most libraries collect old books, maps, newspapers and pictures of the locality, though they will not necessarily be in the branch nearest your home. The local newspaper is likely to have old issues, perhaps going right back to the time when your road was built, which they will probably let you look at if you ask. The vicar of the parish church may help you, for his parish registers could have a lot to reveal about who lived and died in the street – maybe somebody famous? – and so will old street-directories (ask for these at the library). There may be a local history society who would help you.

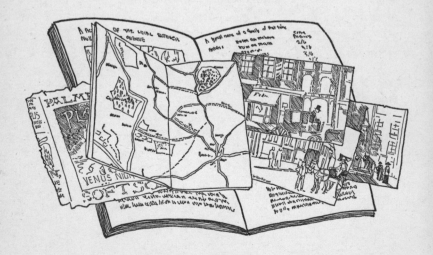

66

I live in a not-very-old road, built in 1875. At my local library, I found and copied a map which showed all sorts of interesting things there before the road came – like farms and footpaths, and a well that supplied the whole neighbourhood with its water, carried to the houses in buckets. I came across a poem about these 'sweet uplands' by Leigh Hunt. Later, I learnt, came a toll-gate, a tavern named after an opera which was popular then, and I found an account of runners who ran races nearby. The library had old pictures of these things which could be put in their photocopying machine. Already my history collection was building up! I wrote to the railway people and they told me about the nearby station which was built in 1868 and a local tunnel which used fourteen million bricks. From the local history society I learnt about the family who had owned the land and through whom the road got its name. Copies of old newspapers and magazines described what it was like when it was first built. A social worker I met told me of a famous actress whose house is now an old people's home – and this, too, I wrote down in the scrapbook which held my collection. It was interesting to discover that the drinking-fountain had been put up in memory of Mr Palmer – of Huntley and Palmer's biscuits – when he died in 1904 (a picture postcard of it went into the book), and to find the advertisement of a local butcher, with a picture of his horse-drawn van, who delivered meat to the street when it was first built. Finally, I painted a picture of my house and put it in too.

This is what I discovered. I wonder what you might find if you started to collect the history of your street – or your school – or your sports club? Plenty to fill a book, sooner or later – or to put up as a wall display.

There are lots of books on how to find out about local history, such as *Teach Yourself Local History* (English Universities Press) or *Ways and Means in Local History* (Everitt, published by the National Council for Social Service).

Every year, all sorts of interesting things happen to you, but how many will you remember later? A collection of mementoes stuck into a series of scrapbooks – one for each year – would make a fascinating record of your life. And perhaps one day *your* children would enjoy looking through them.

What sort of things might you put in your memento book? Well, looking through my latest one, here is what I see:

Holiday photographs and a map of where we went; animals I drew when I visited a zoo; picture postcards sent by friends, or bought; programmes from theatres and concerts; pressed flowers from the garden of a friend we visited; the menu from a restaurant where we had lunch one day; letters from young friends, with drawings round the edge; newspaper cuttings (about a heatwave); some birthday and Christmas cards, and invitations to parties; a picture, from a brochure, of the aeroplane we travelled in; tickets for interesting places we visited; family photos; a leaflet from a museum; picture form the *Radio Times* of an interesting TV programme; the ribbon from a birthday cake.

What other things might go into a memento book?

A bit of fabric from a special dress; a super school-report; a piece of new wallpaper when your bedroom is redecorated; a photo or drawing of your new bike, the school team, a new baby brother or sister; friends' autographs; a list of films you've seen or records you've bought; details of your special birthday-treat dinner; a little bit copied from a specially good book you enjoyed, or its dustjacket; a poem you wrote; jokes or riddles you've heard; some of the other things in this book you've collected – feathers, rubbings, inn signs, grasses, seaweed, etc; a picture from the sleeve of a favourite record; a patchwork of the wrappings from Christmas or birthday presents.

You can make the pages look very decorative by giving some of them pretty borders or headings – painted patterns, or ribbons and braids, or pressed leaves and wild flowers, or tissue-paper cut-outs.

The Victorians were very fond of keeping what they called 'commonplace books': albums into which they glued anything that struck them as interesting – poems, items from the newspapers, and so forth. You could do the same, and it could make an interesting record of what things in your world today interested you most.

Lots of children collect things like miniature cars or toy soldiers, and build (or buy) garages or forts for them.

What about something different which will make a decorative display in your room – small models of animals, birds, musical instruments or little houses. If you particularly like, say, rabbits, donkeys or cats you'll be surprised how many you can find and how

very different they will all be. A friend of mine collects models of hedgehogs, another goes hunting for – hands! Some people collect small shoes, tiny houses, boats or models of vintage railway-engines. All these things can be bought quite cheaply – made of pottery, wood, metal, fabric, onyx, plastic, glass, soapstone, all sorts of materials.

I have a collection of cocks and hens: some are shown in the drawing opposite. I've bought many of them when on holiday, some in shops at home, and others have been given to me by friends who know of my collection and bring me little birds back from their travels.

The big cock at the back, very colourful, is made of raffia and comes from Italy. The red and green tin one (left) is Mexican, bought in a Mexican craft shop; and the pottery one (centre) came from a friend who took a holiday in Poland. The next one (right), from a Spanish friend, is really a jug – it's made of rough white earthenware which I painted myself: water or wine is poured in at the top and out through the beak (the Spanish word for a jug like this is *porrón*). The hen-on-a-basket (left) is made of white 'opal' glass, comes from France, and is an old design, intended as a pot to keep eggs in. Then comes a glass one, Chinese, meant for a paperweight (centre); a yellow silky one which came off an Easter cake (right); and two (in front) which are traditional peasant designs, both elaborately painted in rich colours on black – a pottery one from Portugal and a wood one from Denmark, given to me by friends after holidays abroad. The last one, of a hen and her chicks, is very unusual. It came from Majorca and is a whistle! Ever since Roman times, clay whistles in this and other shapes have been made as children's toys and have not changed in all the centuries that have gone by. Even the colours, red and green on a white background, are just the same.

Some people have collected 'glass menageries': dozens of those colourful little figures made from glass rods twirled into shape while hot and bendy.

Good hunting-grounds for such little figures are Chinese and Indian craft shops, Woolworth's, and souvenir shops.

If you are musical, would you like to start a collection of instruments (and learn to play each one)? There are quite a lot of unusual ones you can find, which don't cost much. Look, particularly, in shops or market stalls that sell crafts of India, Africa and other countries. Here are some of the things you might find.

First, some familiar ones which you can even get at toyshops as well as at music shops – 'penny' whistle, swanee whistle and

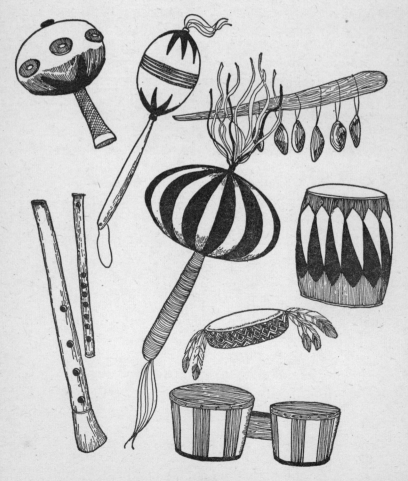

many other types; xylophone; percussion instruments to bang, such as cymbals, gong, triangle, drum; concertina; recorder; mouth organ; 'Jew's harp'.

Then, more exotic ones: African rattles, Japanese shakuhachi (bamboo flute), Mediterranean bird whistles (see page 71), South American ocarinas (pottery wind-instrument), West Indian marracas to shake, castanets and tambourine from Spain, African bongo drums, Indian bells, even a kalimba – a kind of piano from Africa, not very expensive.

There are a number of museums containing musical instruments, or with 'ethnological' collections that include primitive musical instruments. And there are 'folk' records of music played on such instruments.

Here are two interesting books: *Flutes, Whistles and Reeds* and *Drums, Rattles and Bells* (both by Kettelkamp and published by Wheaton). They tell you the origin of lots of instruments – and how to make quite a number, from things as simple as drinking-straws!

Lots of people who started collecting cuttings from newspapers and magazines when they were children found this so interesting that they went on and on for years, filling volume after volume. And if you, too, concentrate on a suitable subject, a collection of cuttings could turn into something really important one day. What starts as so many scraps gradually turns into a valuable reference book which lots of other people will enjoy reading.

THE ORDER OF RELEASE.

So, first of all buy a really large and strong scrapbook which will last. Its pages need to be big because newspapers are themselves big, and although you can chop up columns of text to make them fit, big headlines and pictures still need enough width.

Whenever you stick a cutting in, be sure to write against it the name of the newspaper and the date. Sometimes an item continues on the back of the same sheet of paper; in that case, make a kind of hinge from Sellotape so that the cutting is not stuck down but can be turned over.

What sort of subject might you choose to collect? Here is a list of ideas, but I'm sure you can think of many more:

Tennis tournaments
Cartoons
Earthquakes and volcanoes
Royal family
Ships and sailing events
Celebrities, like singers or actors
Show-jumping
Space exploration
Test matches
Cup finals
Railway news
Dramatic rescues
Crosswords and other puzzles

Fires
Wildlife or zoo animals
Wonderful inventions
Strange and unlikely events, such as flying saucers
Dogs or cats in the news
Storms, floods and gales
Archaeological discoveries
Any foreign country that interests you
Mountains and climbing
Aeroplane news
Ballet

If you have a pen-friend living far away, he or she might find you some that you wouldn't see yourself. In fact, you can get all your friends hunting for you.

Or you could make a funny collection. One of my friends collects crazy misprints (like 'Then add the milk and the butter and rub the mixture well into the floor'); another whose initials are P.C. finds lots of headlines like 'P.C. attacked in an alley' or 'P.C. severely reprimanded'; and a third enjoys finding pictures from one news event and headlines of another (quite unconnected) and putting them together with hilarious results.

(Collecting *old* newspapers is described on page 12.)

If you started collecting unusual pets of all kinds, you might end up with quite a little zoo on your hands. But before you think of getting even one pet, there's a very serious question to ask yourself. Are you quite sure you will *go on* looking after it properly all its life? Daily feeding and cleaning can be quite a bore if you're not really keen. Every pet is a living creature which will *suffer if you neglect it*.

Choose only pets that are happy to live in a confined space. And be sure to get a book telling you exactly how to feed and care for your pet.

Here are some ideas. (Buy them from a petshop, or look in the pages of *Exchange and Mart* weekly.)

Reptiles : terrapins (water tortoises), lizards, grass snakes (these are all kept in a vivarium – a glass tank). *Outdoors :* toads, tortoises, frogs and newts. *From abroad,* so they need warmth: tree frogs, salamanders (axolotls). *See also* pond life, page 36.

Furry animals : rabbits, white mice, guinea-pigs and hamsters you probably know about already. What about lemmings for a change, or fancy mice (deer mice, spiney mice, woolly mice, dormice, etc), tame rats (very intelligent), or gerbils?

Birds : budgerigars, canaries and foreign finches are best. *Outdoors :* pigeons and doves; or bantams (small decorative chickens).

Insects : see page 52.

Fish : see page 36.

If your local petshop hasn't got what you want, you can order most of these (and cages, etc) from Parslows Farm, Common Side, Great Bookham, Leatherhead. Send for information about them and lists of books on how to look after each of them.

Among books which cover all kinds of pets are *Your Book of Pet Keeping* (Risdon, published by Faber), *Inexpensive Pets* (Spoczynska, published by Wheaton) and *Smaller Livestock for School and Home* (Bolger, published by Blandford) – this one covers fish as well.

GERBIL

DUTCH MOUSE

RED CRESTED
CARDINAL FINCH

Picture postcards were first produced in Britain at the end of the nineteenth century. The early ones were much more varied than

most of ours today – with pop-up figures, beautiful actresses hand-painted, royal, patriotic and political inscriptions, embossed ones, and so on. A lot of them had pictures from the First World War, or showed early aeroplanes, trains, ships, etc. Then there were comic postcards with drawings by artists who became quite famous (Phil May and Donald McGill are the best known); and others with songs.

All these you can still find very cheaply in boxes in some junk shops or secondhand bookshops. And if you're really keen you can subscribe to the magazine *International Postcard Market* (94 Idmiston Road, London SE23), through which people buy and sell old cards; or *Postcard Magazine*, which costs 50p for six issues a year (from R. Dale, 123 Balmoral Road, Gillingham, Kent).

Old Christmas cards are a very good thing to collect, too. They began earlier – in 1843 – and soon became very elaborate, sometimes padded or scented, or with elaborate folds, embossed or lacy. Then there are birthday cards – and Valentines.

If you want to collect modern cards, a good place to go hunting is at the bookstalls of museums, where you may find cards of all sorts of things from dinosaurs to antique fire-engines, daggers to dolls' houses. Buy a postcard album for them.

Other kinds of cards you might like to collect: old playing-cards, menu cards, and cards handed out by shops and other trades. Ask grown-up friends to help – and search those junk boxes!

And for a combined postcard-and-stamp-collecting idea, turn to page 99.

A useful little book on the subject is *Discovering Picture Postcards* (Shire).

Posters are a good thing to collect if you have lots of wall space to hang them on.

Old posters from Victorian times (or even later) are now quite valuable, so perhaps some of today's posters will be later. Study the ones you see in the streets, and on stations, etc: which do you like best?

Sometimes, the people who issue these posters are willing to give them away free if you write to them. Travel posters are particularly gay. Local travel agents may be able to help you here, or you could write to the country of your choice – most countries have a national tourist office in London (and some in other big cities, too): just look up the name of the country in the telephone directory and see what you can find.

There are, of course, poster shops in many towns now. In addition, see what museums and art galleries have to offer. For example, the Imperial War Museum (Lambeth Road, London SE1) has reprinted a lot of old posters from the First World War which you can buy for 50p each. London Transport (280 Old Marylebone Road, London NW1) has done the same with early Underground posters, and *Old Motor Magazine* (17 Air Street, London W1) has road transport ones.

Wall charts aren't quite the same but are interesting in a different way: they carry more information as well as pictures. You can get them from the organizations listed on page 111 (free unless stated otherwise).

TEES-SIDE INTERNATIONAL EISTEDDFOD

Over 30 Countries

**Meet the World!
Daily competitive events for folk
singers and dancers,
instrumentalists, brass bands,
choirs and soloists. Evening
celebrity concerts featuring
professional international
artistes.**

PAGEANT OF MUSIC & DANCING

INTER TIE 74 PRISSICK SCHOOL BASE, MARTON Rᵈ
**MIDDLESBROUGH, TEESSIDE
27 JULY - 3 AUGUST**

Further details - INTER-TIE, 21 Albert Road, Middlesbrough, Teesside. Telephone 0642 46601

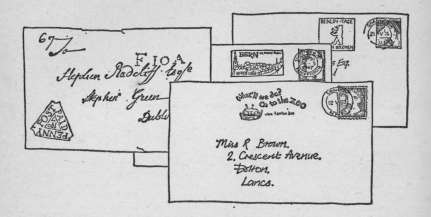

Postmarks are older than stamps. As long ago as the seventeenth century, when private individuals ran delivery services for letters (before there was a Post Office), some letters were marked with a rubber stamp to show the date on which they were dispatched. Later, someone had the idea of adding letters to indicate where they had been dispatched, too. These early postmarks, though rare now, don't yet cost as much to buy as rare stamps, and could be very interesting to collect.

When stamps were invented (see page 98), another kind of postmark came in. Postmasters marked the stamps with a special cross, to prevent their being used twice.

Since then, these marks have been combined and changed in design. And many special marks have been used on different occasions. They may carry words announcing an exhibition or anniversary. Organizations of many kinds – Boy Scouts, Football Clubs and, of course, many commercial firms – have their own symbols or names stamped on envelopes alongside the official postmark.

Did you know you can hand in letters direct to the special mail sorting-office carriages on trains that carry the post between cities? When you do, the letter gets a very special postmark. It might say, for instance, MIDLAND TPO GOING SOUTH. You could take an envelope addressed to yourself to such a train and wait for it to reach you at home, with the postmark.

Collect used envelopes from all your grown-up friends, especially those who go to offices or other business, and you may get a very interesting assortment of postmarks, especially on letters that have come by air or sea from abroad, or from people in the Army or Navy. Keep the entire envelope, not just the mark.

If you want to stick to one particular theme for your postmark collection, here are some ideas:

Seaside towns;
Special anniversaries and occasions (e.g. 'World Refugee Year');
Your own county's postmarks;
Different trades and industries;
Sporting themes;
Air mail marks;
Armed Forces;
Foreign postmarks;
Royal subjects.

You could even collect the marks the Post Office uses to indicate errors – like under-stamped envelopes, wrongly addressed ones, those opened in error, and so on.

When philatelists (stamp-collectors) have conferences, they usually set up a little Post Office with a special postmark. A collection of envelopes with these marks is another interesting possibility.

If you become keen enough to want to join a collector's club, write to the British Postmark Society (42 Corrance Road, London SW5). See also books, museums and magazines about stamps (page 99). And read *Collecting Postal History* (Kandaouroff, published by Lowe).

A 'print' simply means a printed picture, and there are plenty of them about. But when an expert collector talks about prints, he usually means hand-printed ones. The Victorians were very fond of such things, and you can still find hundreds of them in old bookshops and junk shops which you can buy for a few pence. Or you can buy books containing them. You may think at first that they look rather dull – just black-and-white, as a rule, and in an old-fashioned style. But when you look closely you see that there is

often a mass of fascinating detail in them. They were made by a variety of different processes called engraving, mezzotint, etching, lithography, etc, and you might enjoy finding out the differences, how they were made and how to tell one from another. There are plenty of books on the subject.

The Victorians loved travelling and collected prints with views. Some of them were designed originally by great artists, Turner in particular, and you might easily find these. If you were lucky, you might come across some very pretty fashion prints showing the women's dresses of a century ago. Or you could decide to collect birds and flowers, which you might feel tempted to colour yourself. Other possible collecting themes are: rail and road transport subjects, battles, the sea and ships, or theatrical and musical subjects. Some people collect the covers of old piano music.

Victorian Prints (Bedford, published by Cassell) is a good book for a beginner.

If you enjoy cooking, then make your own cookery book by collecting recipes. If you cut them out of magazines, or off labels and packets, or from leaflets issued by food firms, you can simply stick them in – and often these will have colour pictures you can stick in, too. But you will also find recipes in books, or get friends to tell you their recipes, and you will need to write these out yourself in the book.

First of all, you need a suitable book to put them in – not too big. because when you are cooking a recipe from it, it will take up space on the kitchen table. Pages with lines are easier to write on neatly.

Use the first page as a contents page, and write numbers on the tops of all the other pages. Divide the contents page into four quarters, and write at the top of each, 'Meat dishes', 'Fish dishes', 'Sweets' and 'Other recipes'. Then, whenever you glue or write a recipe into your book, put its name and its page number in the right place on the contents page so that later you will be able to look it up quickly when you want it.

Before you put any recipe in the book, make sure it is one that will be easy for you to cook – ask a grown-up if you're not sure. Look at the ingredients: are you sure you will be able to get them all? Some recipes have strange foodstuffs which not all shops stock. Then decide whether it's going to need a lot of hard work and take a long time. Unless you can use an electric mixer, things like beating, whisking and creaming need a lot of energy and patience, and so do sieving, and chopping things up into tiny bits. Don't choose recipes which call for frying in deep fat, or for boiling sugar – these things are a bit risky and could end up in painful burns. And, last but not least, imagine what the finished dish will taste like and whether you will enjoy it or not!

When you are going to write out a recipe from a friend, first make a list of all the ingredients. Be sure to describe them properly (don't just put sugar – should it be caster or granulated, for instance?) and to say what quantity of each should be used. If the recipe calls for baking in the oven, it is important to put the oven-setting down. And always say how long the food should cook.

Here is a list of food firms and other organizations who say they have free recipe leaflets for children:

Atora (suet), Station Road, Daybrook, Nottingham.
Chesswood (mushrooms), Station Road, Daybrook, Nottingham.
Viota (cake mixes), 50 Burnhill Road, Beckenham, Kent.
Robertsons (jam, etc), 50 Burnhill Road, Beckenham, Kent.
Butter Information Council, Salisbury House, London Wall, London EC2.
Apple and Pear Council, Union House, Tunbridge Wells, Kent.
John West (fish), 54 Stanley Street, Liverpool.
White Fish Kitchen, 46 Curzon Street, London W1.
Potato Marketing Board, 50 Hans Crescent, London SW1.
Plumrose (ham, etc), Willerby, Hull.
Australia House, Strand, London WC2.
German Food Centre, 44 Knightsbridge, London SW1.
Norway Food Centre, 166 Brompton Road, London SW3.
Dempsters (cake mixes, etc), 11 Victoria Street, Liverpool.
Scotts (chocolate), Clyde Street, Carluke, Lanarkshire.

All round you are rocks and stones. Not only in the ground but in buildings. Look at ornaments in your home or garden, paving stones, statues, churches, rockeries, station platforms, steps, slate roofs. Look at the coal in the fireplace!

You could start a collection by trying to find samples of the following ones. Common though they are, there's great variety in them to start you wondering just why they differ so much.

Sand: look at it under a magnifying glass: no two grains are the same. *Sandstone:* compressed sand. *Clay:* sticky when it's wet, crumbly when it's dry. *Coal:* black, and made in layers. *Chalk:* white and powdery. *Limestone:* hard, and full of crushed shells and plant remains – you may find fossils in it (see page 43). *Granite:* very hard indeed, black and grey, with a bit of a sparkle. *Marble:* full of veins and streaks, sometimes white and sometimes very colourful, usually highly polished in buildings. *Flint:* this turns up in weird shapes, with a hard, black, shiny interior; it is fun to collect just for the strange shapes if you happen to live in an area where it occurs. (You could make a collection of natural 'statues' in flint, spotting the strange bird and animal shapes that occur.)

SANDSTODE WITH QUARTZ VEINS   CHALK   BROWN BEACH AGATE   SHELLY LIMESTONE   FLINT

These are only a few basic types. To find out all about the hundreds of others there are, you need books on rocks and minerals. You will also need a hammer and a small metal chisel. A magnifying glass and gumboots will complete your kit as a budding geologist.

If you don't live in a district where rocks are visible on the surface, you'll have to look out for quarries, cliffs, road-cuttings or building sites where rocks may be exposed. A few rules: ask permission to go onto private property; never venture into caves or crevices without a grown-up; beware of loose boulders above or below you; find out when the tide is due in if you go along beaches; always tell your parents where you are going before you set out.

Pebbles are bits of rock worn smooth by weather or water, and very pretty some of them are. On beaches in particular you may find stones from which jewellery could be made: rock crystal, amethyst, quartz, onyx, etc. It is possible to buy an electric machine to polish such pebbles, but it costs many pounds, is noisy and has to be left running for days on end. To make pebbles shine you could varnish them (then set them in Polyfilla, if you like – see page 35 – to make paperweights, etc), or simply keep them in a jar or dish of water. Big, plain pebbles could be decorated with poster paint and varnish.

A First Book of Geology (Milburn, published by Blackwell) is very useful. If you want to buy specimens you can't find yourself, write to Duffs (1a Howard Road, Bromley, Kent) or Bottleys (30 Old Church Street, London SW3). If you can, visit the Geological Museum in South Kensington or any local museum with specimens on show. The Natural History Museum (Cromwell Road, London SW7) can send you their *Hints for Collectors of Fossils and Rocks*, and the Geological Museum sells regional handbooks and maps.

There's a simple way of preserving seaweed, and once you know it you're all set to start collecting.

Float the seaweed in water (slightly salted). Underneath it slide the piece of paper you want to mount it on, and below that a flat tin tray or something similar. Then lift up tray and paper with the seaweed on it, and let the water run off. Put the paper and seaweed between sheets of blotting-paper, with something heavy on top, and leave until completely dry.

Seaweeds come in quite a lot of colours, and some very strange shapes. You can guess from its name what Sea Lettuce looks like! The Wracks are a whole family of brown seaweeds with knobbly fronds: Bladder Wrack is the one with air pockets which you can pop. Thong Weed – well, you can guess its appearance from its name: it looks like brown bootlaces. Oar Weeds have big, leathery, brown ribbons – usually you find them only after a storm because their normal place is in the deep sea. Their other name is Tangles: if you swim into a patch of them, you'll know why! Laver is a delicate red one with lettuce-like fronds. Fan-shaped Dulse and Carrageen Moss are also red.

You can either glue each piece of dried seaweed on a separate white card, adding its name and details of when and where you found it. Or you could select several seaweeds to make a picture to frame. Or you could decorate a lampshade or box with seaweeds or put them under transparent plastic to make a table mat.

When you are beachcombing for these, you can also add to your collection of shells (see page 94) and you might also be lucky enough to find other treasures, like a dead starfish or sea urchin.

Among a number of good books for beginners is *The How and Why Wonder Book of the Seashore* (Lamb, published by Transworld).

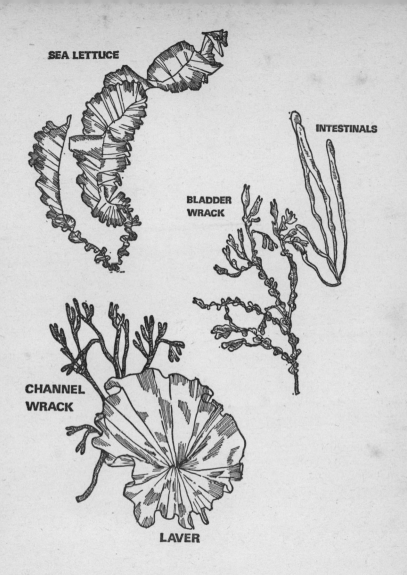

SEA LETTUCE

INTESTINALS

BLADDER
WRACK

CHANNEL
WRACK

LAVER

What an amazing variety of seeds there are: some too small to see, others huge – like coconuts. You can find them after plants in the garden have flowered, in the hedges and countryside, on trees – or fallen from them (conkers and acorns, for example), and inside the grains that farmers grow as crops. In the kitchen, too, you find them: peas and beans are seeds, the pips in oranges and melons and other fruit are seeds, nuts are seeds. Many spicy things were seeds before being ground up: pepper, mustard, nutmegs. Look in a packet of birdseed for other kinds.

So there are plenty of places from which to get seeds for your collection. And if you ask friends going on holiday to bring you back any 'finds', you may get some very unusual ones, too. Natural history museums and some botanical gardens often have fascinating displays, or you can find out more about them in books on plants and trees.

You could glue all except the larger seeds onto sheets of coloured paper to hang up, writing its name against each one.

Or you could use some of your seeds for experiments. For example, line a jar or glass with damp kitchen-paper, and put several seeds between it and the glass. Keep an inch of water in the bottom of the jar. You can observe how long each seed takes to show a root and a sprout.

You could make a collection of plants you've grown from kitchen seeds. Apple pips, and plum stones will do better if you first put them between pads of cottonwool in a jar in the refrigerator for about two months before planting. (Keep the cottonwool damp all the time.) Try orange pips and peach stones if you have central heating, or melons, marrows and cucumbers – these grow into creepers later.

You may collect far more seeds than you need for these purposes, but don't throw them away. You can make marvellous things from them like necklaces, decorated boxes, collage pictures and so on. Seeds can be dyed in coloured ink, painted, sprayed gold or varnished.

Things to Do with Seeds (Selsam, published by Chatto and Windus) explains all about seeds, and tells you how to do experiments with them. My book, *Growing Things* (Piccolo), has a lot about growing kitchen seeds. *Seed Picture-making* (R. and G. Marsh, published by Blandford) is about collages. It shows pictures of hundreds of seeds.

If you take up shell-collecting you can call yourself a conchologist. This is an obvious choice for anyone living by the seashore, but even if you don't there are quite a lot of shells to be had from the fishmonger (scallops, mussels, whelks, winkles, clams, etc) or bought from shops that sell exotic shells. Then there are the shells of lake and river creatures. And what about snail shells?

Not only shell-collectors but shell-fish have fine-sounding names. Among sea-shells there are the chitons (rather like woodlice in shape), the conical whelks and – rather flatter – top-shells, the tent-like limpets, cockles and mussels (these two are bi-valves, which means that the fish has two shells hinged together), the nautilus which is like a spiral, the auger shaped like a unicorn's horn, the long, thin razor-shell and the cowrie. These are only some of the shapes you might find on the beach, in a fascinating range of colours, pale or dark, pearly or speckled, shiny or rough. Some may be so small that only with a magnifier will you spot them among grains of sand. Go beachcombing (particularly after a storm) and you will find them in pools, by rocks or breakwaters, or among seaweed. Around the time of a new moon or of a full moon, when the tides go down very low, is a good period to discover unusual shells – but

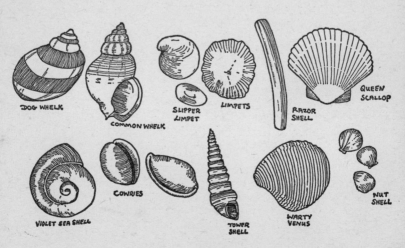

DOG WHELK

COMMON WHELK

SLIPPER LIMPET

LIMPETS

RAZOR SHELL

QUEEN SCALLOP

VIOLET SEA SHELL

COWRIES

TOWER SHELL

WARTY VENUS

NUT SHELL

be sure not to get caught when the tide starts to flow in again. Keep away from treacherous sand or mud into which you might sink.

If you are going to collect shells seriously, then you need one of the many books about identifying, arranging, labelling and studying your finds. But if you are collecting shells just because they are beautiful, you may like to varnish them or keep them in a glass dish of water to show up their colours well. There are lots of things you can make from shells.

A famous shell shop is Eatons (16 Nanette Street, Charing Cross Road, London W1). Nearly every local museum has a shell collection tucked away somewhere. Two good books for beginners are *Discovering Sea Shells* (Charles, published by Shire) and *Your Book of Shell Collecting* (Stratton, published by Faber).

Things to make with shells are described in my *Summer Book* (published by Methuen), which also has ideas for using collections of fir cones, pebbles, pressed flowers, seeds, etc.

Most of us like to bring back from our holidays some little trinkets that remind us of the place we visited. Probably you have seen in friends' homes small china ornaments, for example, with the names of seaside places on them, or teaspoons with the coats-of-arms of holiday towns, or pennants (see page 39). You can collect coloured teatowels or handkerchiefs with views of holiday resorts, and hang them round your room – very gay. Not so ambitious are collections of stickers, or even luggage labels, with place-names on them. Other collectable things you find in souvenir shops are miniature copper things: saucepans, lamps, bells, etc (almost doll-size).

You can collect other kinds of souvenirs, too. For example, if there is a famous historical character who interests you, you could try to make a collection about him or her. Take Nelson, for example. There are lots of places in Britain associated with him: the Norfolk village, Burnham Thorpe, where he spent his childhood; houses where he lived later – in Surrey, Somerset, Devon, etc; his ship (the *Victory*) is on show at Portsmouth; and many museums (in London, Wales, and elsewhere) have Nelson relics. Some of these places sell souvenirs, such as tiny busts of him or models of his ships, others have picture-postcards, and you can always take photos or make drawings to add to your Nelson collection. Shops which sell gifts and little things for tourists may have Nelson trinkets – near Trafalgar Square in London, for instance, you can get small replicas of Nelson's column. Junk shops may have old versions of similar things. You might yourself make some Nelson things out of cardboard, etc – his black eye-patch or his Order of the Garter star (look at a portrait of him for ideas). Soon you will have enough to start your own Nelson museum on your bedroom mantelpiece!

It may be possible to obtain exact replicas of historical documents connected with your chosen hero or topic. Bookshops sell them in kits, under the name of Jackdaws. A company called Historical Documents (14 Rathbone Place, London W1) makes copies on imitation parchment: some branches of Woolworth's sell these.

Replicas of old newspapers reporting historical events are published by Peter Way (28 James Street, London WC2).

You could collect souvenirs of all sorts of people: Dickens, Wellington, Shakespeare, Queen Victoria, Bonnie Prince Charlie (if you live in Scotland) – or, for that matter, fictional characters (even Mickey Mouse or Batman!).

Special events – like the World Cup or Princess Anne's wedding – always cause a mass of souvenirs to appear. When Wolverhampton Art Gallery recently put on a show of coronation souvenirs, they were able to collect together an extraordinary variety of things, beginning with a souvenir medal of 1547 for the coronation of the boy Edward VI. This century's souvenirs of coronations, up to that of our own Queen, included tea-cards, paper flags and decorations, booklets, jigsaws, money-boxes, glasses, horse-brasses (see page 48), beakers, plates, labels and playing-cards. Quite a lot of scope for collecting!

The most popular collecting subject of them all!

The first step is to persuade someone to make you a birthday or Christmas present of a special loose-leaf album, and tweezers to handle the stamps. You'll need some little folded paper hinges with which to stick them in. Oh yes, and some stamps! But you could start by collecting old envelopes from friends and soaking the stamps off. People who work in offices may get lots of foreign ones. Don't throw away any envelope that has an interesting slogan or postmark stamped on it (why not? see page 82).

Be sure your hands are clean before you start putting the stamps in. Write the description in neatly before adding the stamp. Use a different page for each country, or each subject (ships, birds, etc) – this depends just how you want your collection to build up. If you collect by countries, and buy old as well as modern stamps, you can gradually build up a history of that country, its rulers, and big events; and get to know about its animals, crops, industries and peoples through the little pictures on the stamps.

You can collect 'mint' (new) stamps as well as used ones, of course. Rowland Hill, inventor of stamps, wrote that there was 'great bustle at the Stamp Office' on 1 May 1840 when the very first stamps were issued – and it's often like that at Post Offices today when some new stamp appears, to commemorate a special occasion. Such stamps are sold for only a limited period, and therefore soon become scarce. 'First-day Covers' is the expression collectors use for envelopes bearing new stamps issued on their first day and postmarked to prove it. The Post office, and some dealers, produce special envelopes with pictures printed on one side and space for the new stamp on the other, which you can buy in advance of the great day. Then, on the day, you buy the new stamp, stick it on the envelope (addressed to yourself or a friend) and post it so that in due course it is delivered with the all-important date on it. The Philatelic Bureau (2 Waterloo Place, Edinburgh) can send you a free booklet containing information about these.

Another kind of collecting involves matching postcards and stamps (they are called maximum cards). The card's picture matches that of the stamp.

There are scores of books and magazines on stamp-collecting, lots of stamp shops, and clubs to join. You can see collections in the British Museum, the Birmingham Museum and sometimes at others. Many schools start their own stamp clubs, and you can get a colour booklet about how to start one by writing to the Post Office (Publicity Branch), St Martins-le-Grand, London EC1: it has lots of other useful information in it. You might also like to write to this address for wallcharts and leaflets about both stamps and the postal service, or for permission to visit a sorting office in action or the Post Office Tower in London.

But the very best place to start is at the Young Collectors' Exhibition in the National Postal Museum near St Paul's Cathedral (King Edward Street, London EC1). And a good small book for beginners is *Discovering Stamps* (Shire).

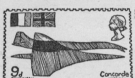 

Anyone can collect travel tickets, you may say! But there's a bit more to it than that. If you get friends to contribute, you might build up a collection, glued in a scrapbook, that covered all sorts of far-flung places. You could draw maps and glue the tickets in place on them, marking the routes in – with the number of miles and how long the journey took, by rail, road, air or ship.

Collecting railway tickets is a serious business these days. Rare specimens from some lines that have closed down are bought and sold for quite large sums, but others from interesting lines (like the Liverpool Overhead Railway) can still be bought for $\frac{1}{2}$p or so. Then there are special tickets – for excursion trains, children's, workmen's, forces on leave, cycles, dogs and prams. There is even a collectors' club – the Transport Ticket Society – with a regular newsletter, through which you can buy and sell tickets (its address is 18 Villa Road, Luton, Bedfordshire).

Later, you might want to extend your collection to other railway things – posters, timetables, uniform buttons and badges (see page 10), whistles, signs, even crested spoons and plates. None of these costs much. British Rail have, in London and Glasgow, depots where such things are sold. All over the country, there are railway preservation societies and museums which sometimes sell such items; and you can also find them advertised in railway magazines.

When you have become as keen as this, you will start reading railway histories (there are dozens of them), talking to railmen, visiting rail museums (over a dozen in Britain) and the Transport Records Office in London. If you live in an important railway town, the library will have lots of 'railwayana'. There are bookshops which specialize in railways (like the Roundhouse at Harrow).

There are masses of books and magazines on the subject, and here's a club you might like to join: British Young Travellers Society, 41 Forest Hill Way, Dibden Purlieu, Southampton. A good book to start with is *Discovering Railwayana* (Smith, published by Shire).

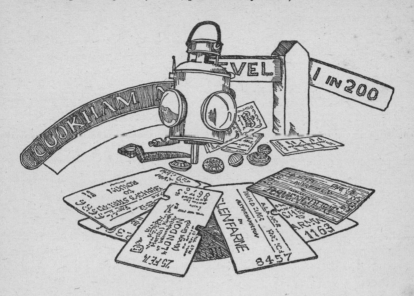

Whatever you collect, the problem may be 'Where on earth shall I keep it all!' The answer may be to start another collection – of interesting little boxes, or of tins.

Old tins are now becoming much sought after by quite serious collectors (and a museum of them is about to open at Reading). Sometimes many pounds are paid for what only a few years ago would have been chuck-outs. Some old tins were beautifully designed and coloured, others have quite a story to tell – like the toffee-tins given by Queen Victoria to all her soldiers fighting in the Boer War one Christmas. Some very old tins still turn up in attics, cupboards and garden sheds.

The first tins, for biscuits, were made by Huntley and Palmer's. Coaches used to stop outside what was then their little shop at Reading to get biscuits for their long journey ahead. Thomas Huntley's brother was an ironmonger, and he started to make tins by hand, to keep the biscuits fresh. It was not until 1870 that tins began to be made by machine, and in all sorts of fanciful shapes (like sentry-boxes or books).

Biscuit and toffee tins are often very decorative today, too, and one day may become quite scarce. After all, many things once packed in tins are now coming in plastic containers, so what you collect today may be a rarity by the time you're grown-up.

Cans – the kind of sealed tin in which you buy soup, vegetables, salmon etc – are not usually so interesting (except for making things with) though you might be surprised, if you started a collection, to find just how many shapes and sizes there are. You can get an interesting book, free, on the history of cans from the Metal Box Co, Baker Street, London W1, and a guide to can sizes and shapes. The first cans were made as long ago as 1812.

If you are too often given toys you don't really want, it's a good idea to let it be known that you're collecting one particular kind – then you may get plenty of additions to your collection, as well as what you buy yourself. Certain toys are made for collecting: you buy one, or one set, then keep adding more. Obvious examples are railways, furniture for a doll's house, small 'character' dolls, or model soldiers.

Do you like building things? Then constructional sets like Meccano or Lego are an obvious choice. Famous Meccano is for the mechanically minded; Lego is more likely to be your choice if you fancy yourself as an architect (though you can be an engineer and make vehicles, too).

There are lots of other kits for model-making – planes, ships, armies, etc – if you're clever with your fingers.

If you've a passion for cars, scale models like Dinky, Matchbox or Solido may be for you. The Solido range has lots of foreign cars, racing ones, some vintage cars, and a great many military vehicles: which will you specialize in? Dinky has ordinary cars plus lots of buses, lorries, etc; they also do planes. Matchbox has all these and bikes too. Corgi, Palitoy and Mattel are other ranges to look out for. Build your own garages and road systems for them.

You could collect puppets – the more you have, the bigger and better the plays you can put on, with the help of friends.

If you aren't sure what to start on, walk round a big toyshop like Hamley's in Regent Street, London, which will give you plenty of ideas; or send for catalogues. But pick something that you will go on enjoying for years, and which has plenty of scope for additions.

Use Blu-Tack, double-sided Sellotape, 'magic mounts' or picture-pins to fix things to walls.

1. Collect some shoe boxes, discard the lids, and fasten to the wall to make display-cases, this way up:

2. Using strong cardboard and wide, plastic sticky-tape for hinges, make a screen to fasten flat things on:

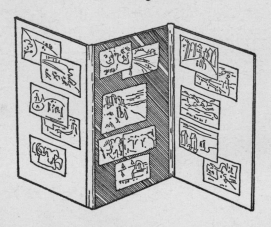

3. Hang a knife-box up sideways to display very small items:

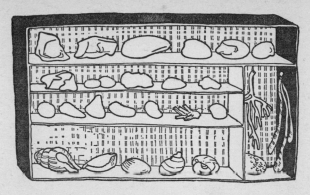

4. Use transparent plastic, plus plastic sticky-tape, to cover a yard of firm material (or card) with pockets and hang this on the wall or a door:

5. Plastic seed-trays make good storage units stacked on top of one another; and marked with self-adhesive labels.

Covering Pots

This is how to make a cover for a yogurt pot – or beaker, lampshade, dish or anything shaped like this:

You can put to good use a little bit of geometry. You need a ruler and some newspaper to make a paper pattern .

First, measure the pot.

Measure across the TOP and divide by half: let's call this measurement T.

Measure across the BOTTOM and divide by half: call this B.

Measure the SIDE of the pot: call this S.

Take B away from T and write down the DIFFERENCE: call this D.

Now for a little simple arithmetic.
Multiply B × S and divide by D. (Call the result X.)
Multiply T × S and divide by D. (Call the result Y.)

To make the pattern, take a sheet of paper and with one end of your ruler at the top left corner, mark off the distance X along one side. Keeping the end of the ruler in the corner, move the other end a little across the paper and again mark the distance X; keep doing this until you have a curved line of marks as in the diagram. Then do the same with the distance Y.

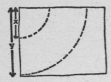 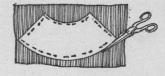

Cut out the curved strip shown by the dotted lines, put it round the pot, and cut off just as much as is needed to cover the pot (allowing for a little overlap). Now you have a pattern with which to cut out the fabric, paper, foil, etc, for the pot-cover.

Glass or paper baubles – as sold for Christmas trees.

Finger puppets – buy or make them.

Odd epitaphs on tombstones, copied into a book.

Wooden spoons and other utensils (you could paint them).

Braid (embroidered ribbon) remnants.

Coloured enamel mugs and dishes.

Clay pipes.

Little baskets, bowls and boxes.

Unusual embroidery stitches – make a sampler.

'Cat's cradles' and other string patterns. (Galt's toyshops have a book of them.)

Coats of arms – draw each in a book. Find out more in books like *Discovering Heraldry* (Shire).

Plastic fruit and flowers.

Candle ends – to melt down and make new ones in jars, with cotton wicks.

Bottle-tops – for collages.

Decorative carrier bags – make a wall display.

Skulls and bones – from the countryside, or from the fishmonger and butcher.

Marbles.

Clockwork toys – broken ones if you're mechanically minded, to mend and perhaps give to a children's hospital.

Fish lures – the colourful and elegant replicas of minnows, etc, which anglers use.

Matchbox labels and book-matches.

Train and car numbers.

Bracelet charms.

Transfers and scraps for scrapbooks.

Beatrix Potter figures (in china).

Photographs, especially transparencies of views and buildings.

WHERE TO GET FOOD LEAFLETS AND CHARTS

Danish Food Centre, 2 Conduit Street, London W1 (leaflets and charts).

Dutch Dairy Bureau, 307 High Holborn, London WC1 (cheese-making wallchart, 15p).

Swiss Cheese Union, 10 Wardour Street, London W1.

Argentine Meat Board, 117 Fulham Road, London SW3.

New Zealand Lamb Bureau, Williams House, London W2.

New Zealand Dairy Board, St Olaf House, Tooley Street, London SE1.

Fyffes, 15 Stratton Street, London W1 (banana chart and booklet, 20p).

Israeli Produce Bureau, 64 Kingsway, London WC2.

Agrexco, 40 King Street, London WC2 (wallchart of Israeli fruit and vegetables, $3\frac{1}{2}$p).

Cirio, 77 High Street, Beckenham, Kent (Italian recipes).

Buitoni, 4 Manorgate Road, Kingston-on-Thames, Surrey (Italian pasta leaflets).

Ceylon Tea Centre, 22 Regent Street, London SW1.

Tea Council, 5 High Timber Street, London EC4.

British Sugar Bureau, 140 Park Lane, London W1 (free leaflets, sugar plantation wallchart, 18p).

Fowlers, Glasshouse Wharf, Blackwall, London E14 (West Indian treacle leaflets).

WHERE TO GET OTHER CHARTS AND POSTERS

Subject	Address
Stamps	Post Office (Publicity Branch), St Martins le Grand, London EC1.
Teeth	General Dental Council, 37 Wimpole Street, London W1.
Eyes	Optrex, 17 Wadsworth Road, Perivale, Middlesex (10p).
How detergents work	Shell Centre, London SE1.
Winter recipes	Alcan, 90 Asheridge Road, Chesham, Bucks.
Meat Cuts Coffee growing (8p) Tea growing (10p)	Brooke Bond Oxo, Leon House, High Street, Croydon.
Bacon cuts	British Bacon Curers Federation, Ickneild Way, Tring, Herts.
Fish	White Fish Kitchen, 46 Curzon Street, London W1.
Milk and dairy farming	National Dairy Council, John Princes Street, London W1.
Butter-making	Butter Information Council, Salisbury House, London Wall, London EC2 ($17\frac{1}{2}$p).
Maize growing	Kelloggs, Box 278, Stretford, Manchester (25p).
Baby care	Heinz, Hayes Park, Middlesex.
Sewing	Husqvarna, High Lane, Stansted, Essex.
China-making	Wedgwoods, 34 Wigmore St, London W1.
Herbs	Chiltern Herb Farms, Spring-Wood Enterprises, Buckland Common, Tring, Herts ($2\frac{1}{2}$p).

INDEX